Startup Your Life

Startup Your Life

HUSTLE AND
HACK YOUR WAY
TO HAPPINESS

Anna Akbari, PhD

St. Martin's Press ⚏ New York

STARTUP YOUR LIFE. Copyright © 2016 by Anna Akbari, PhD. All rights reserved. Printed in the United States of America. For information, address St. Martin's Press, 175 Fifth Avenue, New York, N.Y. 10010.

www.stmartins.com

Library of Congress Cataloging-in-Publication Data

Names: Akbari, Anna, author.
Title: Startup your life : hustle and hack your way to happiness / Anna Akbari.
Description: First Edition. | New York : St. Martin's Press, 2016.
Identifiers: LCCN 2016021590| ISBN 9781250099167 (hardback) |
    ISBN 9781250099174 (e-book)
Subjects: LCSH: Self-actualization (Psychology) | Happiness. |
    BISAC: SELF-HELP / Personal Growth / Happiness.
Classification: LCC BF637.S4 A53 2016 | DDC 650.1—dc23
LC record available at https://lccn.loc.gov/2016021590

Our books may be purchased in bulk for promotional, educational, or business use. Please contact your local bookseller or the Macmillan Corporate and Premium Sales Department at 1-800-221-7945, extension 5442, or by e-mail at MacmillanSpecialMarkets@macmillan.com.

First Edition: December 2016

10 9 8 7 6 5 4 3 2 1

Happiness is not a goal, it is a by-product.

—ELEANOR ROOSEVELT, *You Learn By Living*

Contents

Acknowledgments

A book is a startup unto itself: it begins as a mental spark, evolves significantly (though not always smoothly) over time, and requires the contributions of an entire team to make it a reality. I have been fortunate to have a crew of incredible partners in this endeavor. My agent, Kirsten Neuhaus, of Foundry Literary+Media, is the primary reason this book came to fruition—words fall short of adequately expressing my gratitude for her vision, indefatigable efforts, and unwavering confidence in me.

I'm equally grateful for the clarity and precision of my skilled editor at St. Martin's Press, Emily Carleton, whose enthusiasm and belief in this project made it possible—thank you for championing it and me.

My innovation partner and collaborator, Dan Gonzalez, served as a crucial sounding board throughout this journey. His creativity, curiosity, and unflappable temperament make work feel like play every day. John Flood's thoughtful research assistance far exceeded my expectations; thank you for committing wholeheartedly and patiently diving so deeply into these topics and stories with me.

And finally, I am grateful to my mother, Jean Neibauer: Your parenting philosophy of "open the door and get out of the way" continues to serve me. Thank you for giving me the space to experiment and fail, even without a safety net.

Introduction

Sometime in my twenties, I developed a fear of flying. Not a de-bilitating, can't-get-on-the-plane kind of fear, but a high level of anxiety in anticipation of the flight—which was further exacer-bated when the first bump of turbulence inevitably hit. My mind would race, my body would freeze, and I would prepare myself for the worst. As a kid, the thought that a flight would be anything other than successful never entered my mind. But as firsthand ex-perience and a steady stream of horrifying one-off news stories accumulated in my brain, I came to associate flying—consciously or otherwise—with a loss of personal control.

Control, that elusive thing. Like many high-functioning individuals, I thrive when I'm calling the shots. But in the air, the usual systems are completely unavailable to me—not least, any chance of escape. It's distressing at best, completely paralyzing at worst.

You might say that the years between college graduation and the point at which we eventually pair off and start a family resemble that dreaded bout of turbulence. The pressure of establishing sustainable employment, passable financial security, and a stable romantic relationship is enough to make even the most mature, collected person hit the panic button.

I was no exception. I finished my PhD in the spring of 2008. Too burnt out to make any rational decisions about what would come next, I decided to use that summer to decompress and recalibrate. I slept regularly for the first time in years. I taught a summer school course and took on some part-time consulting projects, but for the first time in my life, I also zoned out. It felt amazing.

Soon, fall arrived, and—since I only knew how to think and operate in semesters—I decided it was time to get serious about sorting out the next phase of my life—hopefully making something of the expensive, arduous preparation I'd invested in for so long.

Of course, my timing was terrible. One glance at a newspaper or television that year confirmed that the financial system was collapsing. And even as I saw it affect various bankers and hedge fund moguls I knew, I considered myself exempt from the fallout. *I'm in academia,* I told myself. *How in the world could Wall Street affect me?* A naïve proclamation, indeed, about a series of events that would leave virtually no industry and few individuals untouched.

So there I was, an eager, optimistic woman with an advanced degree and a mountain of debt, ready to tackle the world—but no one was biting. Academia shifted to a mostly adjunct model, so unless I was willing to move back to Iowa or some equally remote location, finding a tenure-track position would be next to impossible. And the corporate world was no more hospitable. In fact, I quickly found that I had more friends who were unemployed than employed. At least most of them received severance pay and had a bit of savings to cushion their job search. I, on the other hand, was still living like a twenty-two-year-old grad student. The panic button was permanently clenched.

This was the first time in my life that I felt a total lack of control. The world as I knew it was crumbling around me, and I couldn't change it any more than the choices I'd made so far—nor did I want to. Instead, my best recourse was to embrace the situation.

At the time, the spirit of entrepreneurship hadn't yet taken hold in our culture. It wasn't until after 2008 that a confluence of technological advancements and financial circumstances, as well as a shift in how work gets done and how money gets raised, settled into our everyday culture, eventually producing a society of what Silicon Valley calls "everywhere entrepreneurship." And yet, even before it became our default work mode and mindset, I had some entrepreneurial ideas I needed to explore. I became an early adopter: In 2002, right after college and while still in the Peace Corps, I ventured out on my own to start a music foundation. I spearheaded the venture, raised all the international financing, and managed the program during grad school for five years, at which time it was permanently integrated into the local community and supported by government funds (no small feat in an underserved area of the Dominican Republic). Building on that theme and momentum, back in the States in 2004, I collaborated with a classmate while still in grad school to start an arts education platform that matched students of all ages with talented creative professionals in New York City for private lessons.

That company eventually fizzled, but I'd been bitten by the bug. Soon, even my casual social conversations shifted to verbal daydreaming about potential companies and projects. *Wouldn't it be cool if there were a . . .* , followed by rapid-fire brainstorming, popped up in more and more exchanges. I knew I couldn't control the rest of the world, but perhaps I could find my own satisfaction in life as an entrepreneur.

This approach challenged and stimulated me in much the same way school always had. Unlike many entrepreneurs, I loved school. Some find academic institutions limiting—but I found them liberating. School was the only place I'd known where an uninhibited exploration of ideas was central to its operation. Where creative imaginings and conversations about idealized possibilities—not just realities—happen daily. It felt like play, not work, and if I could find a way to replicate and sustain that feeling, I could never "work" again.

While I further nurtured my entrepreneurial persona, I continued to develop and teach sociology courses that deepened my understanding of the world onto which I wanted to project my ideas. I taught courses that explored our sense of identity—everything from the way we look to our relationships with technology. I did research on how we form social connections and what helps or hinders our quest for happiness. I was thriving—intellectually. The rest of my life, however, left much to be desired.

For starters, I was broke. Academia pays very little, and starting your own venture pays even less (at first). Not a great combination when living in one of the most expensive cities in the world. How would I pay my rent? Could I afford that late-night taxi home, or should I prepare for a 3 a.m. subway stroll? Which one of my more "successful" friends would pay for my drink out of sympathy? I also was very single. I couldn't articulate what or whom I wanted, let alone attract it. How could I compete with the hordes of gorgeous women in New York when I wouldn't even want to date myself?

It was time to take back control.

Sound familiar? Even if you didn't enter the "real world" in the middle of an epic financial meltdown, chances are you experienced similarly distressing uncertainty during your post-college/pre-settling-down phase. Turns out, getting your shit together is hard. I was accustomed to hard work—I thrived on intensity and challenge—but the assumption was always that there *was,* in fact, a viable solution. That if I just worked hard enough, I could not only manage, but excel. Suddenly, that did not seem to be the case. Nowhere in my lengthy education did anyone lay out the practical guidelines that would make my life suck a little bit less while I established myself professionally. No one taught me how to be happier along the way. Hard work alone wasn't cutting it. I needed a strategy.

So clearly I wasn't an expert at life, but I was an expert researcher. I didn't have all the answers (yet), but I did have a cognitive framework and academic platform to work from—and, most importantly, I knew how to create something from nothing. I suddenly realized that my years of entrepreneurial "training" were exactly what I needed to improve my everyday reality, and being better at life became my obsession. I researched tools and resources, analyzing them and testing them out on myself. I created personal sociological experiments and repeated opportunities for A/B testing—or strategically playing with variables. Taking a page out of tech startup methodologies, I started with a hypothesis, implemented and tested it, gathered feedback, then started the cycle all over again until I found my own variation of product-market fit.

I realized that the entrepreneurial business approach that had worked for millions of people and companies—the same ideas I'd already been using professionally for years—could also work as a foundation for transforming my personal happiness and well-being. And if it worked for me, I knew it could work for other people.

So I distilled my years of studying, researching, and personal experimentation into a replicable, action-oriented, results-driven approach to living a richer life. Because despite the diversity of our circumstances, we all have, at our core, the same issues, the same perplexing questions: the turbulence of figuring it all out.

I used these processes to optimize any given area of my life, from my manner of dress to my dating habits. Once I had tested each process on myself, I added it into the services I offer through my company, Sociology of Style, which takes an intelligent, systematic approach to image and wellness issues, providing holistic image consulting and life coaching. Sociology of Style allows me to help people reformat their lives and fine-tune their well-being—to flourish rather than just get by. I help people project confidence, gain mental attunement, exercise smarter, refine their eating habits, find a mate, and enhance opportunities for personal wealth. Sociology of Style also supports more intangible pursuits, like creating meaning and generally getting "unstuck." In short, I help people be happier.

During this experimental, entrepreneurial journey, I found increasingly wider outlets to share my incremental realizations—or rather, they found me, as word of my services gained media attention. "I never thought about my life that way" or "that's such a unique approach—I'm going to think about how I _____ differently now" was the overwhelmingly common response. I was asked to write articles, appear on podcasts, give keynote speeches, even give a TED talk. Every few months, I doubled the price of my services, curious where I'd cap out, but I saw no dip in clients. On the contrary, my client base grew steadily, so my rates rose with them. CEOs and successful entrepreneurs began to seek me out. Large, highly visible organizations paid me to fly to their events to give speeches. People were paying attention—and investing real money in what I had to say.

I also worked through these ideas in their most natural habitat: the classroom. While I am entrepreneurially minded, I am also an academic and have a passion for teaching. I first taught at Parsons and the New School, then moved over to New York University, where I taught undergraduate senior seminars as well as graduate classes, mentoring students on in-depth research projects. I used the classroom as an experimental field for my research and theories and enlisted my students as a sounding board. My classes were among the most popular in the department, with some of the longest waitlists. Many students told me that, of their entire academic careers, they were most proud of the work they completed in my class, because it pushed them to reimagine the world and themselves in ways they hadn't previously considered. This led several students to seek out internships with me at my company every semester. I continue to mentor many of those students today, and some have become my employees.

Every day and context was an opportunity to test, observe, implement, and refine—as well as an opportunity to share what had worked for me with more individuals on a similar path. People were coming to me every week to learn how to live a better life, so I knew I was onto something.

The Search for the Magical Book

Early on, I also turned to books—books that promised to make me happier and told phenomenal stories. But while many were charming and inspirational, I couldn't find a single one that gave me the practical tools I needed to pull it all together.

Some "gurus" offer broad, philosophical inspiration, while others give highly specific instructions on how to be happier: meditate, create boundaries, think positively, make peace with your body. Many books out there argue that doing any single one of these actions can radically transform your life. Others hone in on a particular aspect of life (e.g., work), or one particular concept (flow) or problem (depression). And most of the remaining books look at the academically oriented "science of happiness" from a positive psychology perspective.

Most happiness books were written by people I couldn't relate to. People who already had all of life's big challenges figured out—a dream job, a loving partner, financial security, and a happy family. Those books, rather than laying bare the process of change, actually demanded that I—and anyone else still figuring it all out—"read between the lines" to see how their experiences could possibly apply to my life.

So where is the guide for everyone else?

Fifty percent of adult Americans are now single[1] (more than ever before), and those individuals are less likely than married adults to own their homes and have children.[2] Where's the guide for the woman who isn't married yet—or in a relationship at all? The woman who doesn't necessarily have kids—and maybe isn't sure she wants them? What about the person who lives in a studio apartment and is trying to transform it into a home but without financial resources?

Since the Great Recession, temporary positions and contract employment have been on the rise, with 40 to 50 percent of the American population estimated to become independent freelancers by 2020.[3] How about a guide for the people who are struggling to carve an independent career path that looks more like their personal vision? What if they have no idea how to actualize an alternative to a 9 to 5 job?

Fifty-six percent of women are currently dissatisfied with how they look.[4] Where is the guide for the woman who is relying on unsuitable and impersonal fashion magazine advice?

Eighty percent of people ages 18 to 44 have their cell phones with them 22 hours per day.[5] What about the man who feels consumed by social media and email, sleeps with his phone, and can't seem to step off the hyper-connected hamster wheel long enough to hear himself think, never mind meditate?

Where is the thoughtful, strategic guide for that person?

This was the book I needed but couldn't find when I was a single, recent graduate, living in a tiny apartment with an equally tiny budget, full of intellectual promise yet with a lot of unanswered questions—and completely overwhelmed by how to begin and where to seek guidance. There wasn't just one particular thing that was ailing me, and the issues I needed to combat were bigger than the ennui addressed in some books. My quest wasn't about adopting a general life philosophy—though that developed as a byproduct along the way. Rather, it was about systematically targeting and transforming multiple aspects of my life over a prolonged period of time. Directives to "just meditate," "think positively," or "dance spontaneously" simply didn't cut it. I knew that unbridled optimism alone wouldn't deliver the results I was looking for—and it likely won't for you, either.

As an entrepreneur, I learned that one of the best things about startups is their ability to "pivot" quickly—to start over after a failure. Lean Startup guru Eric Ries believes you don't succeed as an entrepreneur because you're a "visionary" or simply because you got lucky and were in the right place at the right time. "It's the boring stuff that matters the most," he argues.[6] Personal success, like professional prowess, is about tinkering with the minutiae over and over again. It's about developing and following the right process, not just having a good idea. And that demands rigor and daily maintenance—far beyond a few positive affirmations.

In a startup, the number of unknowns multiplies daily, and there are no existing patterns or company history to look to for guidance. What do you do when planning is not an option? When control is out of your reach? You isolate the small stuff, experiment constantly, and use the results to lay a more sustainable foundation for the future. You validate your idealized vision by testing it out in bite-sized increments. You see what sticks, integrate it, and move forward—and leave what doesn't work behind. Life, it turns out, is not so different from running a startup.

The good news is you don't need bags of cash to be happy and fulfilled. Nor do you need to be a genius. Life is a business, and like most businesses, you'll experience a series of failures along the way. But if you're savvy, you can apply a scientific approach to creating and managing the life you want. In other words, you can take control of the process before you even know exactly what you're aiming for.

Living your life like a startup is about maximizing flexibility and measuring ongoing results, not avoiding failure or reaching one particular end goal. It's about embracing defeat, analyzing it, and failing up. This book traces stories of entrepreneurial triumph and failure, then applies the lessons learned to everyday life.

Your Life, the Startup: What to Expect

This book may inspire you, but more importantly, it will increase your odds of personal satisfaction. It will help you reclaim control and create happiness by rewriting your story through research and strategy, not luck or daydreaming.

Drawing on startup methodology and inspirational stories from Silicon Valley and beyond, this book teaches you to reframe your life using these core principles and anecdotes. Entrepreneurial moguls like Steve Jobs and Mark Zuckerberg rightly fascinate us. Their meteoric rise is the stuff of modern legend, but their path to greatness often is not as seamless as we might imagine—and their journeys are not so dissimilar from ours.

Since life doesn't always permit you to sit down and read cover to cover, this book offers great flexibility in how it can be experienced. You can read from start to finish or easily jump around from topic to topic according to your interests and needs.

Here's what you can expect:

In Chapter 1, "The Imperfect Prototype: Become an MVP," you will learn the value of reframing your life as a work in progress rather than a final product. You'll learn tactics for testing ideas and actions that allow you to operate with greater confidence and efficacy, and you'll see the value of stripping away inessentials. Less is more, in ways you might not expect.

You'll start to retrain your brain in Chapter 2, "Get Your Mind Right: Optimize Your Mental State." You'll ensure that your thought processes are working for, not against, you. Passion and practicality can coexist, and in this chapter I will teach you how to balance your heart with your head. You'll learn where and when to utilize positivity and optimism (as well as its limits) and begin to edit your mental operation manual.

Take back power and start making your own luck through thoughtful experimentation in Chapter 3, "Outsmart Dumb Luck: Experiment-Driven Decision Making." Nothing is too small or insignificant to test, and this chapter proves that approaching your life like a science experiment always takes the blue ribbon. Plus you'll learn why planning can be counterproductive and why even "failed" experiments are beneficial.

In Chapter 4, "Everything I Need to Know I Unlearned: Disrupt Your Assumptions," conventional wisdom gets the boot. You'll get out of your habitual ruts by putting your personal assumptions to the test and learning what you're taking for granted. You'll turn "knowledge" on its head and avoid the groupthink trap while also shaking up the mental models that shape and control you.

We are social creatures engaged in a perpetual performance,

largely at the mercy of our audience. You'll systematize that validation process in Chapter 5, "Win Every Room: Establish Product-Market Fit." Operating in "beta" mode will help you find the intersection of what matters to you and what resonates with your audience—in all facets of life. You'll learn to impart happiness to yourself and those around you by focusing on not just what you're doing but *how* you're doing it.

The way you deliver your goods matters, whether you're seeking a job or a life mate. In Chapter 6, "Work It: The Runway of Your Life," you'll learn to make the world pay attention. Because let's face it—we all judge. A lot. And if the way you look and what you're saying doesn't resonate, the sad-but-true fact is that people are less likely to listen. You'll also redefine authenticity and clarify its connection to happiness. I'll teach you how to hack your image for maximum power potential: you'll put a little spit-polish on your exterior demeanor, fine-tune the way you present yourself, and see how life shines a little brighter in your reflection.

Our lives are increasingly mediated by technology, and you'll learn to expertly manage your digital identity in Chapter 7, "Go Virtual: Life, Mediated." We'll break down the difference between your "real" and "reel" personas and harness the power of tech-fueled surrogates. You'll learn how virtual spaces can be more than time-sucking, airbrushed facades and can actually be liberating and therapeutic, and offer a chance at a second existence—and deeper happiness.

In Chapter 8, "Hustle and Grow: Bootstrap Your Way to Happiness," we'll dissect your relationship with money and you will learn to live lean—not by pinching pennies but through fiscal maximization. We settle the debate on whether money makes you happier and differentiate between "good" and "bad" money. You'll understand what it really means to bootstrap—and why you should do it—and how hustling is the X factor that will give you the edge.

Partnerships are hard, but the qualities of a good relationship—in business and romance alike—are timeless. In Chapter 9, "The Partnership Puzzle: Be Your Own Matchmaker," you'll learn how to harness the power of partnerships to fuel happiness and success. You'll meet some romantic entrepreneurs who are going rogue and disrupting the current courtship model. I'll reveal the real truth behind our endless search for The One, and teach you how to find lasting relationship flow.

In Chapter 10, "Bellyflop with Grace: The Art of Failure," we explore why giving yourself permission to fall down can be a win. You'll redefine what it means to fail, and we'll look at how you can transform failures into opportunities for growth. A hard-earned comeback can be even better than a landslide victory (I'll tell you why), and you'll learn when to test your limits and how to use patience as your secret weapon.

Letting go is hard, so we often linger a little too long, unsure of when to move forward. In Chapter 11, "Peace Out and Level Up: Make Your Exit," you'll learn how and when to move on. I'll teach you to take charge of your relationship with change and live a life in transition.

How many times have you daydreamed of starting over? Chapter 12, "Hitting Refresh: The Life Pivot," teaches you to flip the mental switch that gives you a fresh start—on whatever scale you need. You'll rediscover how to play and use it as a catalyst for reimagining what's possible. You are the serial reinventor of your own life.

Throughout this book, I've included personal anecdotes and amusing stories, and the book's format follows the "scrum" model, an iterative approach to project management often used by agile software developers. Scrum allows teams to respond to unpredictability and complexity by taking control of projects through short work sprints. In *Startup Your Life,* you will become your own scrum master—the person in charge of moving the project ahead and removing any impediments to reaching your goals.

By creating small, incremental goals, measuring and analyzing their results, and holding yourself accountable, you waste fewer resources while mitigating risk and shortening the time it takes to achieve real, measurable results. So at the end of each chapter, I offer realistic, actionable strategies that allow you to implement and live the chapter's lessons. They're a sort of built-in workbook that you can return to again and again whenever you're in need of a tune-up.

And should you want a refresh on the key ideas covered throughout the book, each chapter closes with the top ten chapter takeaways—write them down, share the ones that resonate on social media, or just revisit them periodically as gentle reminders and motivators.

Personal fulfillment is created, not inherited or earned. And a haphazard search for happiness leads to unpredictable, intermittent results, not sustainable well-being. In this book, entrepreneurial methodology lays the foundation for success while you implement these tactics as the scrum master of your own life. Outside forces feel a lot less overwhelming when tackled systematically and iteratively. There will be turbulence, but when approached strategically, it's all within your control. So buckle up, and let's startup your life.

1.

The Imperfect Prototype

BECOME AN MVP

*A designer knows he has achieved perfection not when there is
nothing left to add, but when there is nothing left to take away.*
—Antoine de Saint-Exupery, *Wind, Sand and Stars*

Kevin was a young ex-Googler working at Nextstop, a travel rec-
ommendation startup later acquired by Facebook, but despite his
relative success, he had an entrepreneurial itch to scratch. So he
started working on his amateur coding skills. One of his ideas was
to create a hybrid of Foursquare and *Mafia Wars*, so he hacked
together a prototype in HTML5 and named it Burbn. It wasn't
fancy, didn't incorporate any aesthetic design elements, and lacked
multiple features. Nonetheless, at a party, he showed the prototype
to some high-rolling investors who agreed to a follow-up meeting

with him. Two weeks later he secured $500,000 in seed funding, quit his job, and started to build out his larger vision.[1]

By the time he showed it to Mike, his eventual co-founder, the mobile web app was already bursting with features: current and future location check-ins, photo posting, points for meeting up with friends, and more. Together, they made it into an iPhone app.

It felt too cluttered, so they decided to streamline and slim down the app. They stripped away all the features with the exception of photo posting, comments, and—of course—the ability to "like" photos. They named it "Instagram," and eight weeks later they launched. Within a matter of hours, it jumped from a prototype with a handful of users to the number-one photography app in the iTunes App Store.

In one and a half years, Instagram acquired 100 million users, and Kevin Systrom and Mike Krieger sold the app to Facebook for $1 billion.

Kevin and Mike didn't have a magic formula. But they did embrace a few key principles: They understood that in order to be successful, you need to focus on and master just one thing. They also recognized that perfection is not the answer. Kevin showed his prototype to investors when it was far from finished—in a state, in fact, that others might have considered embarrassing. It wasn't the final product, but he trusted it was good enough to spark interest.

Your life, no matter who you are, is not unlike the early Instagram prototype. Whatever stage you're at, you should be thinking of yourself as a prototype. But not the kind that must be incubated to perfection before it sees the light of day. If you've ever worked inside a large company, you know that from conception to rollout, product development is a long, costly process that frequently stomps out innovation along the way, to the point where the final product is sometimes irrelevant by the time it finally hits the market. You are not like that. You are a different kind of proto-type: a super-early version called an MVP, or minimum viable product. MVPs are bare bones. They include just the most essential features needed to launch the product and get feedback. They allow for minimal risk, minimal investment, and maximum insight. As an MVP, you're able to explore an idea or a hypothesis and quickly and painlessly figure out if it'll work. You're able to go to market almost immediately and test your reception among a small, targeted group of consumers. Then you can make tweaks and revise as needed before expanding your reach—or scrap the concept altogether. An MVP solves a problem or fulfills a need—even if it's an unknown desire (more on that in a minute). The point of an MVP is to confirm that someone cares about what you're doing before you get in too deep. The key word is validation. You're validating what you think might be a good idea. The MVP phase is the learning phase. Only you're not going through decades of expensive schooling or years of on-the-job training for this education.

Early versions of products are called "beta" versions—a term that acknowledges the product might still have a few bugs—and living your life in beta mode has some significant advantages. Namely, it allows you to stop focusing on the final, perfectly polished outcome and instead explore what you can do in the meantime. I'm not telling you to thoughtlessly try out everything that crosses your mind, but rather I'm giving you a license to experiment and play with possibilities as you refine. Your life is more an abstract expressionist painting than a posed portrait, and once you embrace that mentality, the shape and substance of your life and happiness will transform.

Thinking of your life as a startup will change you in many ways, but first let's establish what it *won't* do: It won't make you a flawless human being. Instead, you're becoming an MVP—a lean variation of a prototype. You're a work in progress, so the goal is not perfection. You're looking to become the kind of person who resonates with others, maximizes opportunities and resources, and generally has their shit together. This means fine-tuning the seemingly mundane, teeny-tiny stuff—like what you eat for lunch or your first-date uniform—until it accumulates into a feet-on-the-ground, wheels-in-motion, functioning product. (More on creating a uniform in chapter 6.)

Whatever stage you're at in life, operating like an MVP will benefit you. After all, you'll never be quite the slick, glossy version of yourself that you dream of being (or try to present on social media: like any Silicon Valley startup, life is not as glamorous as its Instagram account would make it seem). As an MVP, you're constantly gathering feedback, looking for opportunity, and refining your life, at any age. It may sound hard, but in actuality, MVPs have distinct advantages. Whether it's your entire life or a particular aspect of it that is still operating in MVP mode, your unfinishedness can be a competitive advantage. First, MVPs are nimble. In the startup world, it's usually an MVP that showcases the seeds of something truly new and exciting. And rather than expecting flawlessness from day one, consumers are just thrilled to gain early access.

But to look around you, you'd never know that anything short of perfection is acceptable. Every day we're bombarded with airbrushed images, heavily curated social media personas, and viral stories of people doing amazing things—seemingly effortlessly. But just like you, they were once MVPs (and many of them still are, just with great PR). We can all take risks, be bold, "fail" (repeatedly), and invert all the assumptions we've carried forever, especially if they're not serving our needs anymore. Don't think of it as starting from scratch, but rather as creating a new iteration of what already existed with the aid of strategic experimentation and audience feedback. This, not the lightning bolt from the blue, is the essence of innovation.

Sometimes building your "product" requires only some expert storytelling and attractive illusion. In plumbing, smoke tests are used to find leaks or weaknesses to the infrastructure by pushing artificially generated smoke through pipes. In the startup world, smoke tests are also a sort of strength test, only without a physical product. With little more than a website landing page, startups can test out their idea and see if it's worth investing more time and resources into building it out. Potential users may simply submit their email address if the site's description appeals to them and get notified if and when it launches. Generally, if the sign-up rate is high, it's a go. If not, it may indicate that either the product is off—or the company's way of describing it doesn't yet resonate correctly. Regardless, the feedback fuels the direction of the product. It's a way to learn a lot, fast, with minimal investment.

Before raising a $14.5 million funding round, Canadian startup Thalmic Labs executed a highly successful smoke test. The company developed Myo, a wireless armband that allows users to control technology through arm motions and gestures. Many advised against the product, arguing that investors weren't interested in hardware products and instead favored mobile/social software. So to prove their concept had merit, the team at Thalmic Labs released videos demonstrating how the armband works. Online views multiplied, and so did pre-orders: over 30,000 of them, totaling $4.5 million in pre-sales.[2] (There was little risk for the would-be buyers, as they weren't charged until the product shipped.)

This video smoke test proved the demand to investors and also generated an early user base eager to test out the product. It wasn't ready to ship when they watched the video and placed their orders, but the users didn't care. Nor did they expect it to be perfect when it first launched. They were excited about trying out something new—probably more excited than they'd ever been about an overly manicured product that had undergone years of testing.

I've also embraced the quick-and-dirty utility of the smoke test. I began receiving a lot of traffic to my website, but I wanted a way to capture more people who might be interested in my services. I had a "keep in touch" sign-up prompt, and people could contact me directly to learn more about how we could work together, but I needed something less committal—something that would allow me to interact with more people in a brief but meaningful way. So I created and posted a quiz on the homepage, offering personal feedback directly from me for respondents. I initially offered it for free, but when the demand was too high to maintain, I started charging $5—a number low enough to make it accessible to most people but high enough to weed out those who would have no interest in paying for the real product. The smoke test demonstrated both that there was a demand for my approach and that people were willing to pay something for it. That was the validation I needed to invest time and money in a paid video series.

Perhaps the most famous smoke-testing method is Kickstarter. It's basically a platform for largely untested MVPs. Before these projects go into full production mode, founders reach out to the online community with a description of their idea and an invitation to pledge a small contribution toward its development, in return for some kind of gift/reward if the launch is successful. Depending on your donation, you may receive anything ranging from inclusion on the company's email list to a personal shout-out in the credits to a free product once target funding is met. If the project doesn't reach its funding goal, it doesn't receive a cent, meaning it's risk-free for both parties. And naturally, when the product does launch, it is anything but perfect, but users don't seem to mind.

You may recall the now-infamous potato salad project launched by software developer Zack "Danger" Brown. Zack set an ambitious goal of $10 on his initial campaign, and yet he managed to lure in more than $55,000 of backing with an oh-so-clever title ("Potato Salad"), a lackluster pitch ("Basically I'm just making potato salad. I haven't decided what kind yet."), and the promise of saying each $1 backer's name out loud while making the potato salad (how he'd prove that utterance, he didn't say) or allowing them to hang out in the kitchen with him while he cooked. It was a tongue-in-cheek campaign that went viral, and people responded.

So what does any of this have to do with you? Living your life like a startup begins with eliminating as much waste as possible during the MVP phase, while also testing out radically new—or totally off-the-wall—ideas. Run some smoke tests and keep it simple and direct—like potato salad. (Yes, I just told you to become potato salad. Bear with me.) Take your diet, for instance. It's far more than an outlet for transforming your figure. You can experiment with it to see which combination of ingredients leaves you energized and which leaves you in an afternoon slump. Or maybe you'll learn that dairy makes your skin break out (something I learned through some dietary smoke tests of my own). Whatever area of your life you're looking to improve, strip down the relevant variables to just the essentials, then thoughtfully reintroduce each "feature." You'll quickly learn what you need, what you want, and what never should've been invited to the potato salad party in the first place.

But remember that simple and direct does not mean boring. The list of successful Kickstarter projects continues to grow, and some of the most successful barely seemed like bankable ideas at the beginning. Take this list of actual projects: "I Love You Mom" t-shirts, a 9/11 memorial art project, "Puglet" (the first all-pug production of *Hamlet*), and Poop: The Game. Now if you were to bet on which projects would likely succeed, you may be inclined to wager on the first two. But, in fact, Puglet and Poop were the big winners here. We could chalk this outcome up to a commercial appetite for the absurd, or we could recognize that unconventional ideas often capture our imagination in ways that defy logic, earning enthusiasm and support for things we didn't even know we wanted. Like potato salad or a game about poop.

As Steve Jobs famously said, "A lot of times, people don't know what they want until you show it to them."[3] In other words, market research *before* you launch can only take you so far. Sometimes you just have to put something out there, even if it's just a smoke test, before you can get answers. Know when to follow your intuition and try something new, regardless of how unprecedented or out of character it may seem for you.

Unfortunately, you can't try every idea that pops into your head. There's only so much time in a day. How do you determine where and how to spend your time? Who or what gets your attention? Where do you invest your limited energy and resources? Thinking of your life—the tasks, projects, hobbies, and opportunities, both big and small—from an MVP perspective means you don't get buried in long ramp-up phases before you push yourself out there. Faster learning, better results. What you currently think is really important may prove to be inconsequential once you get some feedback. And what may have seemed completely silly at the outset may evolve into something popular or meaningful: Zach Brown's potato salad campaign may have started as a joke, but with the money he raised, he not only entertained people but also created Potato Stock—an entire day of potato-themed fun—which enabled him to donate a chunk of the money to charity.[4] When your life is an MVP, you refine just enough of what's essential, and then push it out into action. All the important learning will follow from there.

Think of this new MVP mind-set as a commitment to eliminating waste—wasted time, wasted resources, wasted energy. You're living lean and working smart. This also means you want to test before you invest, to avoid future waste and a bucket of regrets. This is something we fail to do more often than you might think.

For instance, every year, tens of thousands of students enroll in law school—often for all the wrong reasons. Many do so because it seems like a responsible choice with a good salary (most big-firm positions start at around $160,000), or simply because of pressure from parents to choose a profession that will allow them to secure a "real job" upon graduation. All of these are attractive reasons to pursue a profession, as long as they aren't the only reasons. But depending on the state of the economy, and the number of other people choosing the same path, these reasons may not even hold true.

In its purest form, law school is not just a means to an end. For many who love law school, they see it as an opportunity to write, think critically, debate, and operate in a stimulating environment. Unfortunately, law school is largely not reflective of the daily life of most lawyers—in fact, most law students don't even fully understand what lawyers do on a daily basis. That huge disconnect—between the three years of training and the many, many years spent working post-graduation—is just one of the reasons that so many optimistically choose to become lawyers and feel their choice is validated during the preparatory stage, only to find that they hate the actual day-to-day practice of law (if they can even get hired to do it). Think I'm exaggerating? "Associate attorney" was ranked the number one unhappiest job in America.[5]

Many of these young, debt-ridden lawyers didn't operate like MVPs before leaping into the costly, time-consuming journey that is law school. *Would I even enjoy this life? If I don't enjoy it, could I at least tolerate it for the next several decades, every single day? Would I even want to? And at what cost?* So they stay at their law firms, thinking life will suck less once they make partner. And while that hard-earned accolade provides a momentary boost of happiness, the pressure and tedium of everyday lawyering soon settles back in, and with it misery. (I'd estimate that emotional trajectory somewhere around the same spike/deflate/level-out pattern that winning the lottery has on your happiness. It's generally not sustainable.) And once you reach that level of achievement and financial reward, walking away becomes that much harder. There are more than a few 30-something legal partners already counting the days until they give themselves permission to retire—in 15 to 20 years. Sure, there are some lawyers who love their jobs, but quitting the legal profession (or at least getting out of Big Law) is so widely desired that entire consulting practices have sprouted up, dedicated to helping miserable attorneys get out of the game.

Think of all the things you diligently test out before committing to them. You test-drive a car before you purchase it, and more likely than not you try on clothes before buying them to avoid getting stuck with an ill-fitting garment. In fact, it's possible you think about these micro-decisions—which ultimately don't determine your long-term, sustainable happiness—for far longer than you do bigger decisions that just seem "obvious." Who wouldn't want the chance to make $160,000 their first year out of school?

Before we get in too deep, let's clarify what we mean by *happiness*. I'm talking about subjective well-being, or what is sometimes referred to as *eudaimonia*. Basically, it's human flourishing. It's not a momentary spike of pleasure but a prolonged feeling that you're alive and thriving. True happiness doesn't mean there won't be ups and downs—it's fulfilling to experience a full range of emotions—but we flourish when we're engaged in activities that enrich us. You can't change what you were born into, but you can change how you live your life—and fortunately, that makes all the difference. Becoming an MVP is the first step in redesigning the happiness potential of your life.

So why am I talking about lawyers? Because choosing a career on autopilot is the perfect example of living a *non*-MVP life—and one that makes a lot of people very unhappy. For you, maybe it was choosing medical school. Or becoming an accountant. Or a teacher. All potentially rewarding professions, for the right person. Or maybe you applied this default mindset to finding a mate. I'm not saying you should never make the "obvious" choice (and to be clear, lawyering *is* the right choice for some people), but when you commit to living your life like a startup and transform into an MVP, you're far less likely to invest years and hundreds of thousands of dollars into figuring out that you hate something. You learn it faster, cheaper, and (most of the time) in a more joyful way—primarily because you've (smartly) avoided the years of agony, as well as the accompanying regret. (In the next chapter, we'll work on changing the mind-set that would place you in that predicament in the first place.)

Becoming an MVP might sound like a regression. But in actuality, it's just a stripping away of all the murky matter that gets layered on as you age. It's a return to your core functionality. To why you do what you do, and how best to do it.

SCRUM MASTER CHEAT SHEET

The best possible moment to become an MVP is today. Right now. The timing will always be as imperfect as you are, so choose now. And here's how:

☞ **STUMP YOURSELF.** Who are you, and who do you want to become? What are your life priorities? What are your skills and strengths? What makes you happy? And what makes you miserable? (An important yet often overlooked question.)

Whether you're changing course in your career, considering a geographic move, or just want to feel more alive, asking the obvious-yet-hard questions is the foundational step we often skip, take for granted, or dismiss as fluffy and unimportant. Rethinking your decisions and goals as an MVP allows you to focus on learning all the essential information about yourself—like whether you'll thrive or dread every day—before you find yourself in hard-to-escape predicaments. As an MVP, you're exploring possibilities, not polishing a finished product. The point of an MVP is to validate your idea, to prove that someone cares and that it's worth the investment. And sometimes you're the very person you must prove that to. So think critically about your life and what you want it to look like. What will nourish and sustain you?

☞ **BE YOUR OWN GURU.** Life evolves in unpredictable ways. And sometimes the goals you thought you wanted no longer apply. But it's not the specific goals that matter (*finish graduate school by 25, get promoted to VP of my company, buy my dream house*). Startups can't predict the vicissitudes of their business or industry over their lifetime, but what they can confidently declare is the way they want to operate and what larger ideals drive them. The same is true for you. Companies often have mission statements—a few lines to explain their goals and define what's important—that will endure over time. But instead of creating a wordy, jargon heavy mission statement for your life, I want you to do what Silicon Valley marketing guru Guy Kawasaki suggests to companies: skip the mission statement and instead develop a mantra.[6] It should be brief (only a few words) and get to the heart of what fuels you. It should anchor all the decisions you make—now and in the future. Apple's mantra is "Think different"; Coca-Cola's is "Refresh the world"; Google's is "Don't be evil." (Whether or not you think these companies are living up to their mantras is a different conversation.)

Channeling your inner Zen isn't easy when you're in startup mode. But your mantra will keep you on track when life tries to derail you. Mentally referring back to it is a fast, easy way to check in with yourself. And when repeated over time, it keeps you focused as you evolve toward a particular goal, whatever that may be. You likely won't tell anyone your mantra, but you will utter it silently, or just let it hover in the wings of your mind while you go about your day.

Remember how Instagram initially stripped down its offering to push out an MVP with just one core feature? Well the mantra is your "one feature." It's that one essential thing that remains consistent, even if everything else is in flux. It drives to the heart of who you are and why you get up in the morning. Be your own guru and let the mantra anchor you.

☞ **COZY UP TO IMPERFECTION.** Kickstarter campaigns can be awkward. The promotional videos are of varying degrees of professionalism, the accompanying landing pages may offer little functionality, there are few bells and whistles, and the product you're looking to buy doesn't even exist yet. But these campaigns also open the door to ideas and projects that often get stopped up by all the bureaucratic boundaries of life. Take the *Veronica Mars* Kickstarter, for example. A complicated combination of ratings, budgets, and scheduling led the CW network to cancel the cult-favorite television series in its third season. Bereft fans advocated for a film finale, so the show's team launched a Kickstarter and met its $2 million goal in just one day, ultimately ending with a total of $5.7 million.[7]

This smoke test found a hugely receptive audience, and the film was able to move forward without restrictions.

Walt Disney is credited with saying, "The way to get started is to quit talking and begin doing." So what keeps us from starting and doing? Often all that pre-doing jabber is rooted in a fear of failure, embarrassment, and imperfection. Fortunately, as an MVP, you accept all of those as part of the process. MVPs don't look fancy and polished, and they often have a lot of "bugs"—the technology equivalent of human quirks. The bugs are eventually worked through, and the product runs more smoothly as a result. But the startup doesn't stop operating during that time. MVPs trade perfection for ingenuity, slickness for savvy, diversification for flexibility. As an MVP, you're not lowering your standards, you're simply moving the end goal.

☞ **TRIM THE FAT**. Most of us have a lot of blubber slowing us down. Not literal cellulite or even the inevitable life scars we like to refer to as "baggage," but rather the heavy weight of all the "shoulds" and "musts" we force upon ourselves: *I* should *like yoga. I* must *be with someone at least 6 feet tall.* Layer that with the default ways we often mindlessly operate, and it's easy to realize why we often feel immobile, trapped. This extra weight pushes us further and further from our core mantra. It's time to slim down and shed everything but the essentials. You can gradually add things back into your life, but perhaps for the first time in a long time (or ever), approach each decision as minimally as possible, from the small (your workout routine) to the big (your choice of mate). Ask yourself what you actually enjoy (the answer may be less accessible than you'd imagine), and commit to just catering to that for a while. No, life isn't always simple, but it's impossible to move forward if you're buried under unnecessary complexity. Time to get back to basics.

THE LAZY LOWDOWN: TOP TEN CHAPTER TAKEAWAYS

1. It's never too early or late in life to be an MVP.
2. MVPs are exciting and nimble, giving them a competitive advantage over "perfect" products.
3. Test before you invest (and remember: sometimes smoke tests are best).
4. Eliminate waste before it crushes you.
5. Get rapid feedback—from yourself and your audience.
6. MVP is a learning phase. Make it your permanent phase.
7. Be your own brand of potato salad: sometimes wacky is both wonderful and wise.
8. Challenge the "law school default" mindset.
9. Sometimes happiness and practicality don't coexist, so embrace happiness and redefine "practical."
10. Return to your core. Or discover it for the first time.

2.

Get Your Mind Right

OPTIMIZE YOUR
MENTAL STATE

Since you alone are responsible for your thoughts, only you can change them.

—PARAMAHANA YOGANANDA, *Where There Is Light*

Jordan went on a wilderness adventure in Alaska at age 23. During a prolonged period of heavy rain, he decided to climb a summit in the Brooks Mountain Range, eventually finding himself at the top of a mountain, alone. In that moment, he experienced a spiritual awakening in which he recognized his own smallness and declared his commitment to living a life of consequence. From then on, it was this combination of humility and a desire to serve that anchored all of Jordan's decisions. He didn't know where those decisions would take him, but he now had a personal philosophy on which to base them.

Jordan went on to optometry school, still unsure of how his calling would manifest. He signed up for a medical mission to Mexico, where he worked with individuals who were vision impaired. Jordan realized that one boy, who believed himself to be blind, was actually severely myopic. He outfitted the boy with the proper glasses, which allowed him to see clearly for the first time. Jordan now had a means to both contribute and express himself: by bestowing sight. That was his mission. He just needed to figure out how to replicate it in a scalable, sustainable way.

Through more trips like the mission to Mexico, in conjunction with more schooling and independent research, Jordan Kassalow founded the Scojo Foundation, which eventually became VisionSpring, a social enterprise that designs and distributes eyeglasses globally to people in need.[1]

I'm not sharing this story to suggest that you need to go on a charitable mission or start a foundation. I share this story as but one example of a successful mindset. While we may roll our eyes when people tell us success is "all mental," adopting the right mind-set is often a key differentiator—not only in determining success but also happiness. And this isn't just about advocating positive thinking (though science shows it can be powerful when applied correctly—more on that in a minute). Transforming the way your brain processes ideas and assesses opportunity can reset the stage for every decision you make. Think of your life as a "Choose Your Own Adventure" novel, and the mind-set you bring to those decisions as the factor that determines your fate.

So what do I mean by mind-set? You're probably thinking of the personal affirmations, gratitude practices, and meditations recommended in other books. And while those tools are terrific and often effective, there's another piece to the puzzle that's often ignored.

What are the mental qualities that make an entrepreneur successful? Any guesses? An extensive study indicates that 98 percent of company founders surveyed believe a lack of willingness to take risks is a significant obstacle to launching a company.[2] If you are completely risk-averse, you'll never take the plunge. But what builds and motivates that appetite for risk varies. Some, like Jordan Kassalow, embrace risk because their quest is rooted in a drive to change the world, or because they experience some sort of spiritual awakening. Others start from a place of "nothing to lose" and hedge their bets accordingly. But that doesn't mean risk can or should only appeal to those extremes. A little risk is beneficial to everyone. Unfortunately, the very concept is often misunderstood.

The list of prominent thinkers and doers who endorse risk-taking is too long to mention. All the way back in the first century, Seneca taught that "there are more things that frighten us than injure us, and we suffer more in imagination than in reality."[3] Winston Churchill allegedly divided the world into optimists and pessimists: "The optimist sees opportunity in every danger; the pessimist sees danger in every opportunity." But perhaps spiritual author Neale Donald Walsch sums it up best: "Life begins at the end of your comfort zone."[4]

So if our wisest philosophers embrace risk, why is it still such a dirty word?

Let's first dispel the myth that risk always means recklessness. Though it may seem counterintuitive, "playing it safe"—however that translates into your life at different moments and contexts— is sometimes a far riskier choice than taking a leap. Why? Because avoiding risk at all costs often leaves us in the hazy, dangerous position of never making a decision at all. How many times have you heard someone say they're mentally "stuck"? Fear. Worry. Inertia. These feelings slowly eat away at our happiness, and even our self-esteem. Getting stuck is often an attack of what poet Shel Silverstein so aptly referred to as the "Whatifs": a parade of worries that invade your brain, even when things are going well—things like being struck by lightning, being poisoned, or growing green chest hair.[5]

Okay, so maybe you don't lie awake worrying that green hair will begin to grow on your chest. But this type of "catastrophizing," as they call it in psychiatry, is paralyzing. Refusing to make a change might feel like a safe decision, but simply staying the course provides a false sense of security. We too often believe that the status quo will always be the status quo, despite abundant evidence to the contrary.

And it's not just people who become stuck in this fearful mindset. How many large corporations and industries were disrupted by young, aggressive startups, all the while ignoring the obvious shifts in the air? Think Blockbuster, or the taxi industry. Times change. People change. Needs change. *We* change. But sometimes we need to get out of our own way before we can move forward.

But if the whatif army of fears keeps us from moving forward, what motivates us to push beyond them?

One factor is passion. As a society, we're passionate about passion—and I'm not talking about the sexy bedroom variety (though that can be equally incentivizing). We want to be passionate about everything we do, and we're told it's our right. Our jobs, our hobbies, our life goals, what we eat for breakfast—our passion for passion knows no bounds. That passion can push us beyond our comfort zones to pursue our dreams, to take the risks necessary for success.

But should it? What is a healthy amount of passion when it comes to optimizing your life? How much passion allows you to thrive, and what's the tipping point into a passion pit? Every good entrepreneur needs passion to succeed, but the most successful understand that it must be balanced with strong practical applications.

Shai Agassi had a vision: He wanted to free the world from its dependence on oil. He wanted to make electric cars more affordable and improve their charging capabilities. To actualize that vision, he founded the company Better Place in 2007, and his charismatic personality and compelling vision helped him raise (and spend) upward of $900 million in venture capital—without ever demonstrating any real, sustainable, scalable results. So how did he win that sort of backing, if not from traction or progress? Good ol' passion. Shai Agassi was the darling of investors, world leaders, and celebrities alike, making up for what he lacked in hard data with an endless supply of motivational speeches.

Don't get me wrong: it's great to have a big idea, but if you believe your own hype without nailing down the details needed to realize that vision, then you will eventually crash and burn. Agassi was a futurist who presented his personal beliefs and ideas so effectively that passion trumped practicality and blinded him to the difficult realities of his business. By 2012, Better Place had an operating loss of $386 million, and in 2013, it filed for bankruptcy and was liquidated.[6]

Agassi is definitely not the first leader to bask in vision at the expense of reality. Sometimes what makes a founder so great at their job—big ideas and an even bigger personality—is also their downfall when it comes to getting the company from point A to point B. When the company began to run out of money, Agassi was replaced as CEO. This sort of leadership change happens often. Founders of successful companies often start out as the CEO only to find themselves replaced—whether the company is doing well or not. Why? Harvard Business School entrepreneurship professor Noam Wasserman identifies multiple ways in which founders may become blinded by their own passion: they are unable to see flaws, verify customer demand, or identify potential future pitfalls; they expect the best and therefore don't plan for the worst;

and they believe their sincere desire to change the world will guide them to success.[7] Sometimes, as with Jordan Kassalow and Vision-Spring, the formula works. Other times, as with Shai Agassi and Better Place, these passion-induced blind spots can mean that founders eventually find themselves out of a job.

Sometimes, though, a change in leadership is just a natural, need-based evolution of the company rather than a failure on the part of the founder. After all, one person can't play every role forever, no matter how driven. That's why many founders are not just one-trick ponies but serial entrepreneurs. They have more than one great idea over the course of their lifetimes, and after contributing to any given project to the extent of their abilities, they move onto something else. Sometimes it's similar, sometimes completely different. But the core formula remains the same: identify a passion, match it with an existing need, develop a strategy, and allocate resources.

So how can passion and practicality coexist?

I received my MA in a program called Liberal Studies. Not sure what that is? You're not alone. The degree expands on the liberal arts we often study as undergraduates and provides more depth into interdisciplinary fields like the humanities and social sciences. Did you miss a few key literary classics in college? Need to brush up on your Enlightenment philosophers? Do you have a penchant for cultural criticism? Then this masters program might be for you. I knew it was perfect for me the minute I read that it promised to produce "public intellectuals." Because I didn't just want to be a stuffy academic, I wanted to be an intellectual of the people! I wanted to think deeply about everyday issues that mattered to everyday people—and wouldn't it be great if I had two years to talk and write about these topics with other like-minded folks? I practically skipped to the first day of class.

A Liberal Studies MA is an example of what's called a "terminal degree." In other words, you can't go on to get a PhD in it. So from a career prospects perspective, it leaves its graduates in an interesting place. Many of my peers were nonfiction writers of some sort, so the majority had already accepted their nebulous place in the future job market. I, however, had aspirations of going on to get my PhD. Which begged the question: in what?

Keeping the interdisciplinary theme, I initially gravitated toward programs like American Studies and Performance Studies, both of which were fitting homes for my proposed dissertation topic of "the semiotics of visual self-presentation and its connection to power" (see why it was confusing?). But before I applied and enrolled in one of these programs, I did some research. I contacted a recent grad of one of the programs for insight. Turns out she loved the program but was finding it difficult to find faculty positions in other departments and was starting to wish she'd focused within a single discipline, then gone on to teach in an interdisciplinary department. Basically, if you came from something more traditional (like economics or anthropology), people understood what you did. If you came from one of these newer disciplines, finding a job became more challenging.

So I made my way to sociology, where I still developed an interdisciplinary dissertation project while anchoring it in sociological methods and theory. It was a compromise that felt true to the topic I so passionately wanted to pursue, but still allowed the creative freedom I desired, without compromising postdoctoral hireability. Win-win.

Steve Jobs is attributed with the instruction to "follow your heart, but check it with your head." It's not either/or. It's both/ and. Just not always simultaneously. Sometimes one follows the other, other times they shift positions of prominence. But a good rule of thumb is to make sure both your head and your heart are invited to the party. We too often choose one over the other at the expense of both.

Passion, practicality, and positivity—the three P's—all play key roles in determining whether our minds are working for or against us. Trying to shut out or over-rely on any of them is not a recipe for success. But understanding how they influence your thoughts, emotions, and behaviors will lay a more balanced foundation for future decision-making.

First, back to passion. Psychologist Dorothy Tennov's research concludes that when romantically involved—when passion is spiking—we may operate in a state of "limerence," or infatuated love, that can last from 18 months to three years.[8] During this phase, our thoughts and actions may be extreme, obsessive, and irrational. Affairs with nannies, dalliances with prostitutes, crimes of passion—the tabloids are riddled with shocking examples of behavior that defies logic. In other words, passion often overrules practicality. So how do we safeguard ourselves and our relationships against the power of passion?

I encourage my clients to develop a ten-tenet (or whatever number feels right) rulebook to guide their lives. In my practice, this starts with them taking an open-ended questionnaire that helps them to identify where the pain points are in their lives— from email overload to money worries to family issues. They also ponder their longer-term goals and what's currently helping or hindering peak happiness. This kind of free-form contemplation allows us to isolate what's working and what isn't and build a conscious, sustainable lifestyle around it. Once they've considered their optimal way of living, we work backward to create their rulebook. I ask them to consider: What does it take to get there? What habits or behaviors are inhibiting progress or creating roadblocks along their path? What boundaries need to be created?

Which ones need to be torn down? And as a result, they identify their rules to live by. Some may be motivational: *Taking the time to properly nourish myself honors my body, fuels my mind, and positively affects everyone I encounter.* Or perhaps it's a reminder to keep things in perspective at times of stress: *Holidays are my time to formally express gratitude to the people I love for the role they play in my life.*

No two rulebooks look alike, and they vary greatly in length and style. But they all serve as day-to-day guides as well as emergency plans. So when crisis—or passion—strikes, you need only refer back to your rulebook to make decisions and move forward. In other words, the decision may not already be made for you, but figuring out what to do becomes a lot easier when you have an established rulebook to follow.

This also keeps your mind—which is so easily influenced by everything from emotions to hormones to food to outside stimuli—in check. Your life rulebook allows you to make logical, practical, fast decisions so you can respond quickly and confidently whenever there's a new choice or challenge. The rulebook takes the pressure off and provides a roadmap for dealing with and optimizing each challenge as it arises.

Rules around relationships are particularly important, as the flood of hormones we feel in the lust phase is akin to being high on some very potent drugs. Suffice it to say your judgment needs all the help it can get. The goal is not to extinguish the fires of passion and make matters of the heart a routine checklist. But you can strike a balance between passion and practicality by mindfully laying out what's healthy and satisfying for you before your head is clouded by a sexually charged fever or an impulsive inclination. What is it you seek? What brings out the best in you? The infatuation phase can make a delayed text reply or a canceled date or an inevitable disagreement that much more emotionally charged. But taking a moment to mentally reassess the situation in light of your rulebook allows practicality to soothe passion's delicate temperament. They should be allies, not adversaries.

As a society, the only thing we love as much as passion is positive thinking. We're taught that positive thinking is the pathway to, well, pretty much everything. Anchored by the rise of *The Secret*, the controversial book and film that promotes positive thinking for radical life transformation, popular psychology trends would have us believe that telling ourselves "we can do it!" is the key to achieving all our hopes and dreams. Wouldn't it be amazing if it were that easy? Unfortunately, positivity, while wonderful and important, is a bit more complex than that.

First, let's understand the facts. Cultivating regular gratitude does have a measurable effect on your happiness. Optimists are physically healthier people (and they live longer). And negative thoughts significantly deteriorate your well-being by limiting your options and putting you into survival mode. Positive thoughts and emotions, on the other hand, expand your worldview and your imagined possibilities, which in turn gives you the space and mental capacity to sharpen your skills and acquire new resources.

But is there a downside to all this pervasive positivity? Yes, and it's called "optimism bias." Consider it from an entrepreneurial perspective. We all know the majority of new business ventures fail: that number hovers somewhere between 50 and 80 percent, depending on our definition of "failure" (a topic we'll explore in a later chapter). Regardless, it's a sizable chunk. And yet, over 80 percent of entrepreneurs—the same number who are likely to "fail"—believe they have at least a 70 percent chance of success.[9] So despite the data that says the odds are not in our favor, we bet on ourselves. This is both occasionally necessary and potentially dangerous.

If it's any consolation, large-scale organizations are just as prone to this type of gross overestimation as individual people.

For example, the initial cost estimate of the 2012 London Olympics was 1.8 billion pounds, which later became 4.2 billion, then 9.3 billion.[10] You might think this sort of wild miscalculation was an isolated event, particular to the London games, but in fact it is largely the norm, not the exception, when it comes to the Olympics. As one analyst pointed out, the bids are drawn up to win votes, not to accurately reflect the financial realities of the project—which, if we ever admitted them ahead of time, might scare off half the suitors.

Entrepreneurs are also guilty of this deliberate misrepresentation. They have to be. Statistics are not on their side when it comes to short-term economic gain. The first few years are often very difficult: high stress, low earnings, and no real sense of security or promise of what's to come. But it is that irrational belief that they will be the exception that allows a few stars to eventually succeed—right?

I once met a man who professed to having a "negativity shield": whenever anyone said something he deemed negative, he'd swipe his hand over his face, a gesture intended to block the poisonous words slapping him in the face and accosting his mental perspective. Aside from the socially awkward and potentially insulting nature of this peculiar practice, a "negativity shield" is about as effective as a "pessimism magnet" (the best never-produced product in *SkyMall*).

Yet simply believing we're above average is something many intelligent, mentally healthy individuals do. So is it necessarily a bad thing?

In less scientific terms, we could rename optimism bias as "lying to ourselves": *Smoking won't kill* me. (Two-thirds of smokers die from smoking-related illnesses.[11]) *BASE jumping* [think superhero wingsuit flying] *is just a fun, harmless thrill!* (One in 60 participants dies. Yes, dies.[12]) Unrealistic optimism can heighten our appetite for risk, but it's not just the big, obvious stuff we're prone to misconstrue—we also lie to ourselves about small stuff everyday, which isn't always a bad thing. It's part of how we get through the day. *I think I successfully covered up that blemish. He probably lost my number.* Thinking positively in these situations allows us to keep moving forward and focus on other, more pressing concerns. But it's when we slip entirely into either lying to ourselves or resigning ourselves to defeat prematurely that we get into dangerous territory.

Though it may look similar, optimism bias should not be confused with confidence. And it's also different from good old-fashioned positivity. But avoiding optimism bias while maintaining a positive outlook is not simple. Take marriage. People love to casually throw out the statistic that 50 percent of marriages fail. But that's not actually true. Since peaking in the 1970s and 80s, the divorce rate has been on the decline.[13] Even if "'til death do us part" is the only marker of a successful marriage, at the current rate, two-thirds of marriages will be divorce-free winners.[14] Of course, there are a number of factors that explain our shifting partnership patterns (to be explored in a later chapter), but the marriage naysayers persist. After all, it's easier to avoid taking the plunge by believing that the institution of marriage is inherently flawed and sets you up to fail, or by clinging to an outdated stat that doesn't take a nuanced look at modern relationships. Whether your marriage endures has far more to do with other factors within your control than national statistics. The institution of marriage is not conspiring against you. But looking at nuance takes work. (Just like marriage.) And it's far easier to put up a negativity shield or become the marriage scrooge than it is to accept your own responsibility—and more optimistically, your personal power—in realistically controlling the outcome of that partnership. That's not an attempt to convince you to get hitched. Rather, it's a way of nudging you to rethink how optimism and practicality can "consciously couple."

But here's the surprising twist to optimism bias: It can actually push you harder to reach those goals and prove yourself right. Studies show that effort actually increases with higher levels of optimism, particularly among the entrepreneurial set.[15] Thus, success (however we choose to define it) becomes a self-fulfilling prophecy. This is not to say (or endorse the idea) that you should believe the impossible and it will come true. But rather that an emotional and psychological investment in an outcome does spark more dedicated work, which in turn has a real effect on the results and, in turn, your well-being. It focuses you. It begins to permeate your discussions. You start to link other seemingly disparate events and people with this desired outcome, and you find a way to connect the two. It's the work (whether conscious or unconscious) that you do as a result of mentally committing to the seemingly unrealistic outcome that helps you to get there. Not merely the positivity itself.

I am not discouraging optimism bias—in part because you can never completely eradicate it and because it's an important part of taking on calculated risk. When kept in check, it can give you an edge. But I am telling you to maintain some objectivity. Always ask yourself how much you are willing to risk, and don't let your passion induce irrationality or think positivity replaces effort.

SCRUM MASTER CHEAT SHEET

How can you encourage your heart and head to play nicely together? Here's a plan to keep your brain working for, not against, you:

☞ **INTERROGATE YOUR PASSIONS.** Most of us can easily run down all the things that qualify as "passions" for us: food, music, fitness, social causes. But passion doesn't always equate with practicality, which makes the misguided advice to just "follow your passion" incomplete and problematic. Finding the most sustainable place in your life for any given passion requires some thoughtful interrogation. Take an honest look at the reality of your life circumstances and talents, in relation to those things that get your fire going. What skills and resources are needed to power your passion? Does it require additional training? Funding? Outside support? Imagine you're an investor looking at a new startup pitch. Try to find as many potential holes and pitfalls as possible. If it proves problematic, that doesn't mean you need to abandon the passion parade for something you don't enjoy. But just being aware of your weaknesses and possible hurdles will help to prepare you for suboptimal outcomes and increase your chances of dealing with them, rather than letting them derail you until you eventually give up. Whether it leads to a new profession or just a weekend hobby, interrogating your passions is a practical way of keeping what you love in your life for the long haul.

☞ **RETRAIN YOUR BRAIN.** Science tells us that our brains—the way we think and make decisions, our personalities and behaviors—reach a relatively fully formed state by the age of 25.[16] If you just read that and you're under 25, you may suddenly feel pressure to mold your brain as perfectly as possible before you abandon all hope at the stroke of midnight on your twenty-fifth birthday. And if you're already over the 25-year-old hill, you may be thinking you're screwed. But fear not! While our brains become a bit more stubborn after that age, they can still transform—with a little massaging. One of the best ways to keep the brain fresh and nimble is to repeatedly introduce new challenges. Yes, you could take up Sudoku or become a crossword master, or enlist any number of brain training apps out there. But that might feel like homework. Instead, make brain maintenance part of your lifestyle by actively implementing new mental and physical challenges into your life. Gravitate toward anything that shakes up your usual routine and that your brain can register as a novelty, especially things that fully engage the senses and require strategizing. Learn a language, pick up some new dance moves, learn chess (hint: refer back to your passion list and use it as a guide wherever possible). Your brain is elastic, so start stretching it.

☛ **WRITE YOUR RULEBOOK.** You've got your mantra—that brief phrase that philosophically anchors the way you live your life—but how do you apply that to everyday decision making? Be clear with yourself about your own rules. If you're not sure where to begin with your rulebook, consider creating an affirmational statement in relation to each of these core areas of life I use with my clients: nourish, spend and save, connect, reflect, polish and present, move, organize, give back, enrich and enjoy, dream. For instance, for "move," you may say, *"I think of exercise as a gift of self-love, not a chore, because it positively transforms my brain and makes me mentally and physically stronger."* Or, if that feels too structured, create your own core categories and jot down the corresponding key concepts you want to mentally guide you, regardless of whatever curveball comes at you.

Perhaps you want to find a way to give back, but feel short on both money and time. So develop a rule that calls for thoughtful spending and combines connection and altruism. *There are small ways of giving back that won't break my back or my bank account; I will embrace them with strangers and loved ones alike, not only on special occasions but in everyday encounters.* Or maybe it's as simple as "find a way to pay it forward every day." Or perhaps "enrich and enjoy" and "dream" fall through the cracks for you. Develop a rule that not only gives you permission but makes it mandatory that you respect those needs. Over time, you may discover another category or area in which you need to create some rules, but don't worry about anticipating them all up front. And remember: Sometimes rules are meant to be rewritten.

THE LAZY LOWDOWN: TOP TEN CHAPTER TAKEAWAYS

1. Getting your mind right starts with getting out of your own way.
2. Transform your relationship with risk.
3. Reject inertia by keeping the whatifs at bay.
4. Introduce your head to your heart, and vice versa.
5. Remember the three P's: passion, practicality, positivity. Indulge in all three in moderation.
6. Let your cup runneth over with realistic optimism, not delusion.
7. A compelling vision alone can only get you so far.
8. The right mind-set is the foundation for your key ingredient: doing the work.
9. Your brain: use it or lose it.
10. Lay down the laws of your life and let them—not your shifting emotions—sway you.

3.

Outsmart Dumb Luck

Diligence is the mother of good luck.

—Benjamin Franklin, *The Way to Wealth*

Jennifer met Jennifer in business school. They were entrepreneurially minded young women on the lookout for new opportunities when they both noticed something: even a woman with a closet full of clothes wants a wardrobe refresh for important events (lest anyone on social media see her wear the same thing twice). And a startup idea was born.

But it wasn't business as usual. The Jennifers didn't immediately break out the spreadsheets and create a business plan. Instead, they staged a series of experiments to test their hypotheses:

Hypothesis 1: *Women will rent special occasion dresses.* This was a big guess. Historically, renting clothing was a sort of last-resort option—and certainly didn't seem luxurious. Would women recoil at the prospect of wearing a dress other women had already shimmied into?

Experiment: To test their theory that greater variety trumped the stigma of renting, the Jennifers hosted a trunk show with borrowed dresses and invited female undergraduates at Harvard to attend.

Results: One-third of the attendees rented dresses. And not only did they rent them, but they also returned the rented dresses on time and in good condition.

The experiment proved that women would in fact rent—and care for—dresses, while also illuminating other valuable information like popular styles, designers, and price points. So they used that data to develop their second experiment and test another variable.

Hypothesis 2: *Women will rent dresses without trying them on.* They had their eyes on Internet rentals as the end game, so confirming that the affordable accessibility of variety outweighed the desire to try before you rent was key.

Experiment: They hosted another trunk show, only this time the attendees were not allowed to try anything on. However, they did enhance their offerings by featuring more of the most popular styles, based on results from the first experiment.

Results: 75 percent of the women rented dresses.

Wow. 75 percent. These were great results. Would 75 percent of women soon turn to the Jennifers for all their party fashion needs? More questions needed answering first.

Unfortunately, hosting trunk shows isn't as scalable as the Internet—you can reach far more people digitally than in person, and shows can't be timed to everyone's individual event needs. The Jennifers wanted to offer the dresses online to reach the maximum number of customers, but it wasn't simply a matter of listing those chosen styles online: What happens when you go from renting something in a party-like atmosphere (everyone's doing it!) to renting in solitude? How does your behavior change? And what happens when you not only can't try it on, but also can't see or touch the dress in person and must solely rely on a digital image?

These were huge questions, and answers required more experimentation.

Hypothesis 3: *Women will rent dresses online.*

Experiment: Launching an e-commerce site takes time and re-sources, so before investing too heavily in an unproven concept, the Jennifers took a makeshift digital approach: they sent a PDF of dress options to a sample group of women who had asked for more info about the company on their site's landing page.

Results: 5 percent rented a dress.

At first glance, declining from 75 percent to 5 may seem like a total failure. But 5 percent was enough to prove their concept could work, given the breadth of the audience.[1]

The company, of course, is Rent the Runway (what Tech-Crunch calls "Netflix for designer clothes"[2]), founded by Jennifer Fleiss and Jennifer Hyman in 2009. And they've come a long way since their first trunk show. Rent the Runway now offers over 50,000 dresses and 10,000 accessories from 200 designers to 5 million bedazzled customers, with revenue expected to top $100 million in 2016.[3] The Jennifers didn't rely on traditional business models or luck to reach those impressive numbers. Instead, they used two macro-trends, the democratization of luxury and the rise of the "sharing economy," which favors access over ownership, as a foundation, then staged experiments until they were certain they could satisfy a pervasive customer need: new clothes on a limited budget for special events.

Entrepreneurs like the Jennifers don't have the luxury of

long-term planning or an analysis of the company's past perfor-mance. All they have is a series of untested hypotheses and lim-ited resources with which to test them. And while a hypothesis is essentially nothing more than an educated guess, it's still a lot more than luck.

Luck. That might be my least favorite word. Anyone who's ever had his or her success or happiness dismissed as "luck" knows what I'm talking about.

If you believe luck is something you're simply born with (or, more likely, without), science is not on your side. Psychologist Richard Wiseman's research found that people increase their "luck" by consciously following four basic principles: they notice chance opportunities, make decisions by listening to their intuition, project positive expectations that become self-fulfilling prophecies, and exercise resilience.[4] In other words: so-called lucky people seize the moment, are decisive and positive, and always find a way to bounce back. Most importantly, these are all active choices, meaning "luck" is generally not something that happens to us but something we deliberately create.

What does this mean in practice? It means that envisioning a reality and thinking positively is just the beginning. Do you think Rent the Runway—or any other startup, for that matter—was suc-cessful merely because the founders had a "vision" and sat around thinking positive thoughts all day? As we've already established, positivity *is* important. Having a vision *does* matter. It's good to know what you want (or what you think you want), and use that as a sort of guiding light. But a positive vision alone will not de-liver results. I promise.

Instead of relying on luck, these companies experimented. They formulated hypotheses and tested them out. They understood that experimentation is the best path to clarity and sustainability. And experimentation isn't about chance. Calculated experimentation yields far more valuable results than years of planning. It seems counterintuitive, but it's true.

And yet, we associate the very word "experimentation" with risk and recklessness. Planning seems like the sounder route. So let's imagine what might have happened if the Jennifers had spent months developing a business plan, fine-tuning it to theoretical perfection, pitching to investors, and then launching a company based on unproven plans. They may have misjudged the styles that women were most interested in, or applied a price point that was too high or too low. They might have been forced to accept input from a series of investors, without the experimental data to demonstrate the validity of alternative choices. All of those missteps might have diluted their vision. Chances are, they would not be the thriving enterprise they are today without experimentation.

While planning *seems* like the responsible choice, it will only get you so far—and it can actually be counterproductive. Planning assumes that the variables aren't changing, that the environment is controlled. But let's face it: that isn't my life and it very likely isn't yours. It was impossible for the Jennifers to foresee if and how women would rent dresses, what their preferences would be, whether they'd follow the rules and return them on time, and if there was a value proposition for designers to lend out their wares. So instead of planning, they had to experiment or perish.

And this is what I'm asking you to do, though it may seem contradictory to the notion of success you've embraced until now: I want you to *stop planning* and *start experimenting*.

Our reluctance to experiment often stems from the fear of public humiliation—yet another case of self-sabotage by the what-ifs. What if I make a wrong move? There's a sense of security associated with maintaining the status quo, even if it isn't serving you or has adverse effects (yes, this is the clichéd-but-true "devil you know" default response). And chances are, many of your potential experiments—the things you might like to try out—may yet seem a bit half-baked. This is a challenge larger, more established companies deal with all the time. Like you, they've got skin in the game. There's exposure. There's plenty to lose. But even megacorps find a way to experiment toward something better.

Take a little company called Starbucks. It boasts over 23,000 locations and $16 billion in revenue.[5] And yet, despite its size, experimentation is still one of its core practices—though likely in ways unbeknownst to you.

In 2008, Starbucks released a list of stores it would close in order to accommodate a dip in performance.[6] One of those locations was a Starbucks in Seattle, its hometown. The following year, in July 2009, another seemingly independent coffee shop opened in its place. The site was 328 15th Avenue East, and the new store's sign read "15th Avenue Coffee and Tea," with "Inspired by Starbucks" written beneath it. Soon, another Starbucks in Seattle closed and Roy Street Coffee and Tea opened in its place.

What was happening? Was Starbucks losing ground in a city whose veins once raced with their venti brew?

Unlike Starbucks, the new shops focused on local food purveyors, a "mom and pop" vibe, and also sold beer and wine. "Hip, versatile, and chic" best describes what quickly became local hot spots. And yet, appearances were deceptive. This was not a return to the quirky charm of independently owned local shops. Rather, these shops were Starbucks-owned "stealth" locations, and despite the fact that they sold coffee and tea, the similarities pretty much ended there. The businesses aimed to match the neighborhood, not the Starbucks brand—which meant no mermaid cups or Starbucks cards. This was a covert experiment in unbranding.

Many thousands of pour-over coffees and two years later, the 15th Avenue secret Starbucks reverted back to a regular Starbucks—sort of. The new decor stayed, now accented with visible Starbucks branding, the food remained locally sourced, and they still sold alcohol. It was Starbucks again, only better.

Starbucks refers to these stealth locations as "learning environments" for testing out innovative concepts and products. It's their attempt to refine and enhance their offerings without starting over. When you're as big as Starbucks, it's easy to just focus on the macro, like revenue and expansion, and coast on "good enough"— for a while, anyway. Eventually, too much coasting and not enough persistent experimentation catches up with even the most powerful companies. Because demand is fluid. Desirability changes. And it's the constant tinkering that keeps companies fresh.

As a result of the secret testing, focus shifted from simply churning out coffee store clones to producing beautifully unique, locally inspired experiences. Experimentation doesn't just help us create something from nothing; it also inspires us to reimagine the possibilities of what already exists.

Experiments don't always deliver the results we want. So don't judge those results on their face value. Remember: Rent the Runway's adoption rate fell from 75 percent to 5 percent when they shifted to digital distribution. But 5 percent, while lower, was statistically significant in that new context, and the insights gathered from negative feedback were essential to the company's development. In your own life, opportunities for experimentation abound, both personally and professionally. For instance, you might experiment with the way you describe yourself and your experience on your resume while interviewing for new positions. Perhaps you'll create a few different versions and send them out to prospective employers. And while a low response rate isn't ideal, it's a useful indication that something is off—because "failure" leads to learning. It provides an opportunity to understand what went wrong and reframe what you're doing, making your next round stronger and smarter than your prefailure attempt. So rethink your understanding of what makes something a "win" when it comes to experimentation.

Of course, experimentation—and "failed" experiments—are anything but new. In the mid-nineteenth century, New England was, in many ways, the Silicon Valley of its time. In fact, Menlo Park, New Jersey, was the site of many inventions, much like its namesake in Silicon Valley. Only, instead of Internet companies, the area attracted the thinkers and inventors of the age of the telephone.

The electric lightbulb had existed for around 50 years by the time Thomas Edison got to it. But Edison—the most prolific inventor in American history, amassing 1,093 patents over his lifetime[7]—knew it could be better. The existing versions were dim and inefficient, so he sought a way to create one that was bright, long lasting, and affordable. No small feat. In fact, it proved so challenging that he tested 300 versions before landing on the first commercially viable incandescent lightbulb.

Edison is called the Wizard of Menlo Park and the greatest inventor who ever lived—despite the thousands of failed experiments he conducted in his life—because that testing eventually led to triumph. He is the champion of tireless, indefatigable empirical research. He is also perhaps the single greatest source of inspirational quotes on the value of persistent experimentation: "There's a better way to do it. Find it." "I haven't failed. I've just found 10,000 ways that won't work." And most famously: "Genius is one percent inspiration and ninety-nine percent perspiration." While it's unclear which of those quotes might be apocryphal, we do know he said this to *American Magazine* in its January 1921 issue:

> I never allow myself to become discouraged under any circumstances. I recall that after we had conducted thousands of experiments on a certain project without solving the problem, one of

my associates, after we had conducted the crowning experiment and it had proved a failure, expressed discouragement and disgust over our having "failed to find out anything." I cheerily assured him that we *had* learned something. For we had learned for a certainty that the thing couldn't be done that way, and that we would have to try some other way.[8]

For Edison, experimentation was just as much about eliminating the wrong ways as identifying the right ones. Using Edisonian logic, each experiment, regardless of the outcome, is necessarily a victory unto itself.

Many of my own experiments have taken this frustrating yet enlightening course. Years ago, when I first dipped my toe into the online dating world, I took the path of many first-timers: one paved in mistakes. At first, I didn't post a photo (I know, I know), then realized I needed something to intrigue and engage my potential suitors. So I uploaded an artistic, blurry shot that didn't quite reveal my identity but rather set an aesthetic tone. Knowing full well that no one would contact someone they couldn't see, I decided I would use the digital platform to seek out individuals I wanted to meet (rather than let them choose me). Once I found a profile that appealed, I sent them a message that explained that I was a professor and therefore preferred to keep my image private (everyone online has some perceivable excuse for their shadiness, right?), but offered them my first *and* last name and a link to my personal website, which had multiple current photos and a bio. I knew most people didn't even offer a first name in their initial messages, and it was nearly impossible to tell if they were real, so I congratulated myself for being so clever and transparent and waited for the result of what seemed destined to be an online dating homerun.

Or not.

No one responded to me. Not one. I followed up again with a few guys, giving them even more information about me. Crickets. Ouch.

Sometimes silence is the most resounding feedback you can receive. While I thought I'd outsmarted the system, I was actually not playing by its rules. It was a case of "too much, too soon." Turns out, people didn't want my full name, website, and links to photos on the Internet via a private message right away. Why not? One possibility I came to consider was that it indicated I wasn't "in it" the same way they were. Not posting photos or revealing information on my profile meant I either thought I was better than them or had something to hide (or both). It also bypassed the textual flirtation and introductory niceties of most initial online dating message exchanges. I wasn't participating in the banter or the digital eye-batting. My approach was completely lacking in subtlety and demonstrated a shallow understanding of the world in which I was trying to operate.

Obviously, this was not my desired outcome. I couldn't believe I'd missed the mark by so much. But that misstep corrected my path in a way I might not have uncovered—at least, not so rapidly—had I taken a more subtle approach. By making distinct, deliberate choices and receiving such strong, instant feedback, I was able to parse out the variables and dissect the outcome. As a result of the tweaks I made, I not only received responses to my messages, but those messages led to a string of great first dates—which then advanced me to the next phase in the process and ushered in an opportunity for a series of stronger, better, more successful follow up experiments. (More on the entrepreneurial nature of dating and relationships in a later chapter.)

Maybe you've been in a situation like this—one in which you are a fish out of water. Or one in which your initial instincts and behavior lead you astray. You can't inherently know what's optimal in any given situation, but you can figure it out quickly through the simple process of *observe, hypothesize, test*. Here's what's key: it's not the immediate success or failure of a test that matters. It's what it teaches you and how it affects your decisions in the future. Each experiment is merely a piece of the puzzle you'll use in other yet-to-be-determined tests. It's something most of us do instinctively, but consciously going through the experimentation process accelerates the rate of learning and allows us to analyze the results more effectively.

So start small and begin observing and testing now. Don't get held up by overthinking before you act (remember: *plan less, experiment more*). I'm not suggesting that you should move mindlessly through space, but remember that "lucky" people manufacture good fortune in part by acting on their intuition—not through inaction. And while leaping before you think is never advisable, remember that these are small or at least gradual changes, not anything that might get you fired, bankrupt you, or lead to a breakup.

Perhaps you've heard the word *biohacking*. It is exactly what you'd think it is: hacking your own biology. Though you may associate hacking with evildoing, most hackers are just computer programmers who tinker with code. They build and rebuild software and hardware to make it better, enhancing it beyond its original purpose or capabilities. And when you mix the hacker mentality with biology, you get a growing subculture of biohackers—the most prominent of whom is Dave Asprey, a.k.a. the Bulletproof Executive.

Two decades ago, Asprey was a 300-pound multimillionaire. While his Silicon Valley career was flourishing, his mind and body were anything but thriving. He was exercising regularly and didn't overeat, but his weight problem persisted, which led to other physiological imbalances. He was mentally foggy and his concentration waned. He felt sluggish, lacked energy, and, most acutely, wasn't happy.

He understood the hacker mentality well and recognized that technology and our bodies aren't so dissimilar. They are both enormously complex with ever-expanding data sets ripe for analysis—and experimentation. So, over the next 15 years, Asprey spent $300,000 of his own money to stage hundreds of experiments on his body. He took body scans and did blood work, tested his nervous system, and studied meditation. He monitored his brain waves, heart rate, and eating habits to a degree that most of us can't fathom (he even installed a brain wave–monitoring machine in his home office, which he used to monitor the effects of the food he ate on his brain and mental performance). He quantified his life instead of just letting it happen.

As a result of his obsessive, technology-fueled experiments, he transformed his body and mind: He lost 100 pounds without restricting calories or becoming a triathlete, he increased his IQ by 20 points, and he energized his mind and body on less, more efficient sleep. He went from being successful and unhappy in his twenties to feeling and performing better than ever in his forties. In short, he mindfully upgraded his life.

Asprey eventually turned his personal journey into a thriving business. His podcast tops the iTunes charts with over ten million downloads, he has a bestselling diet book, and he created and trademarked Bulletproof Coffee (essentially coffee with butter in it), which is a growing viral sensation. His experimentation paid off. Big time.

But fret not: you don't have to become a famous guru or even "bulletproof" to reap the rewards of experimentation.

No matter where you begin or what obstacles you encounter along the way, it's the strategy you hone and deploy—not luck or expert foresight—that allows for radical self-transformation and perpetual self-optimization. It's triumph through trial and error, not certainty. You can diligently pay attention and experiment your way to success. Your life is an ongoing experiment, but it need not be a constant gamble.

SCRUM MASTER CHEAT SHEET

Dust off your hacker hoodie—it's time to create your own luck through experimentation. From Edison to Asprey, there's no single method for experimental success. But there are some general basics that can help. Here's your quick reference guide for launching your own life experiments:

☛ **SCOPE OUT THE SCENE.** We overlook much of what stares us in the face each day, but observation is important. So start paying attention. Whether it's dress habits or technology etiquette, observing the patterns, rules, and modes of conduct in any given space is enlightening. *What dominates? What's missing? Are there any outliers? What's rewarded or punished?* It's easy to get swept up in the rhythm of a situation and take the details for granted. Take a mental step back and observe as objectively as possible. Even if it's a space you've operated in for years or decades, chances are you've never looked at it with the eye of a scientific observer. Take it all in; become a keen observer of your own life and spare no detail. Jot down notes if that helps, otherwise just sharpen your eye and tune into things you've overlooked or taken for granted.

Remember that people don't always say what they want or believe—often what they say is dictated by social norms. Watching humans behave and respond in the moment, "in the wild," is most illuminating. Make a habit of tuning in to the scene around you, and soon your life will be in a constant state of experimentation. Your observational awareness will permanently turn on and become your default mode of operating.

☛ **HEDGE YOUR BETS.** You've seen, you've contemplated, now experiment. Experiments start with a hypothesis. To put it in startup language: you need to validate your idea.

Testing your hypothesis may seem intimidating at first, but give yourself permission to go for low-hanging fruit—like small domestic details—to start. (Don't test out your relationship with your boss on your first go around.) Nothing's too mundane for experimentation. The main goal is just to get yourself in testing mode so that it becomes a less formal, more natural part of how you operate. Prioritize your experiments based on what has the highest potential for improvement and the most positive impact on your life, or simply what bothers you the most. This is about what makes *you* happy—and only you can decide what that is.

☛ **SHOW ME THE MONEY.** How do you know if it's working? Since we're dealing with nuance here, it's not always immediately obvious. No one's going to show up at your door with a giant check, and you probably won't get a marriage proposal this week (sorry). So identify some incremental goals that can serve as checkpoints along the way to these larger milestones.

Life doesn't stop and wait while you analyze your data. Implementation happens live, in real time. But that doesn't mean there's no place for thoughtful reflection and deliberate action. Check in with yourself periodically: *Where am I at? How do I feel? Are there any changes?* If things haven't gone entirely as planned (which is highly likely), reflect on the speed bumps you're encountering and consider some potential workarounds you could incorporate. Look for trends in your results and never lose sight of the fact that each experiment is part of the bigger picture.

THE LAZY LOWDOWN: TOP TEN CHAPTER TAKEAWAYS

1. You make your own luck.
2. Vision without action falls flat.
3. Experimentation beats planning.
4. Follow the formula: *observe, hypothesize, test* (repeat).
5. Long-term change evolves from the small and not-so-trivial moments.
6. You're never too big (or too old) to experiment.
7. Negative results are sometimes the best results.
8. Each outcome is a piece to a larger puzzle—not an end in itself.
9. Tinkering breeds competence, which will make you happier.
10. Remember: science is better than luck.

4.

Everything I Need to Know
I Unlearned

**DISRUPT YOUR
ASSUMPTIONS**

*Whenever you find yourself on the side of the majority, it is time
to pause and reflect.*

—MARK TWAIN, *Mark Twain's Notebook*

The BlackBerry was once so popular—and addictive—that it was
nicknamed the "Crackberry." The little flashing light and real-
time email notifications signaled the user's 24/7, in-demand status, especially back when cell phones were not so ubiquitous. In the
1990s, BlackBerry ruled the smartphone category, and by 2009,
Fortune named it the fastest-growing company in the world.[1] But
just a year later, it started to decline. Companies like Google and
Apple became competitive threats, and the release of the Apple iPad
in 2010 created a demand for touch screens (not the QWERTY
keyboard of the BlackBerry). In a single year, BlackBerry's U.S.

market share dropped from 24 percent to 9 percent, eventually plummeting a total of 90 percent and claiming just 3 percent of the market by 2013.[2]

In addition to the new touch screen technology, consumers also preferred the operating systems on these other devices, while BlackBerry lacked the multimedia interface and app capabilities. Laser-focused on the customers who first enabled their rise to the top—corporate employees—BlackBerry underestimated the full suite of features that regular people would want from their phones. Ultimately, consumers were interested in mobile entertainment technology, not just email machines.

Almost overnight, BlackBerry became a one-trick pony, refusing to accept that private consumers, not corporations, would drive the smartphone market, and failed to innovate accordingly. Ignoring macro-trends in the naïve hope that nothing will change will eventually catch up to any product or company, even an industry leader.

BlackBerry's fall from grace is a lesson in what happens when we refuse to acknowledge change in the air around us and become stagnant. And believe me, it's not just large companies that suffer this fate.

You may have heard the buzzy word *groupthink*. Our society is currently fixated on the value and benefits of collaboration, but groupthink is a different, less beneficial strain of collaborative thinking—one that creates more setbacks than opportunities. It is a type of acknowledged conformity, a rationally justified consensus. But consensus is good, right? When everyone is agreeing on a particular way of behaving or a series of choices, it's easy to think that you're doing the "right" thing and believe that you are less vulnerable to an error in judgment. And even if you do have doubts, the group can quickly erase those from your mind—a sort of inadvertent brainwashing that stops you from thinking critically about other possible scenarios that may help or hinder you. When there's a dominant line of thinking that is perpetuated and rewarded, diverse opinions often lose traction, which diminishes creativity and limits the outcome for everyone. Not to mention that whenever we believe there's just one way of thinking or doing something, we become complacent. And no one wins at anything—including life—through complacency.

Large companies are notorious for falling into groupthink, especially when they're making good-faith attempts to collaborate. Often there's a prevailing mind-set or way of doing business that became dominant at some point in time—either through strategic testing or because of a leadership preference—so it's still accepted as the singular way of thinking and operating potentially years later. Employees who disagree may self-silence to avoid rocking the boat or, worse, risking their jobs. Perhaps you've worked in a place where the groupthink stagnation is palpable, and yet no one's telling the emperor he's not wearing clothes—it seems easier (and safer) to just pretend he is. From corporations to cults, groupthink can have real, large-scale consequences when allowed to run rampant, and entire cultures, not just groups of individuals, can fall victim to the seductive herd mentality.

Startups, however, tend to take a different approach. Groupthink is seen as a liability to avoid at all costs; invalidating assumptions and turning the status quo upside down is rewarded and encouraged.

The first Blockbuster opened in 1985, and by 1994, Blockbuster and Viacom had joined forces in an $8.4 billion merger.[3] Then, in 1997, Reed Hastings's $40 late fee at Blockbuster disgruntled him, and a year later he founded Netflix. Blockbuster was offered multiple chances to purchase the young Netflix for only $50 million but declined. The home movie tide was changing, however, and not in Blockbuster's favor. Customers no longer wanted to walk to their local video store—home DVD delivery was far more appealing, and even that was short-lived with the rise of digital content accessible on personal devices. And yet, denial remained the default Blockbuster mind-set. Despite Netflix's rapid growth and Blockbuster's precipitous decline, Blockbuster's CEO continued to reject any suggestion that they were headed for bankruptcy or that Netflix had anything to do with it. By 2010, Blockbuster was valued at just $24 million[4]—half of what they would have paid for Netflix back in 2000. Three years later, Blockbuster announced it would close all its remaining doors.

Like BlackBerry, Blockbuster refused to accept and adapt. Had Blockbuster listened to market trends and customer demands, it might have acquired the once-tiny Netflix and remained at the top of the movie-rental game. But a failure to transform its offering and delivery mechanism forced the company completely out of business. Blockbuster was like the toddler with his eyes squeezed shut and his hands pressed firmly over his ears, refusing to acknowledge the changing world around him.

This extreme rigidity is often birthed by the most pervasive type of groupthink: conventional wisdom. Despite having "wisdom" in the name, conventional wisdom has a history of stupidity, particularly when it comes to game-changing technology. In 1876, telegraph giant Western Union initially dismissed the telephone as having too many shortcomings to be taken seriously. In 1946, Darryl Zanuck of 20th Century Fox was quoted as saying that television wouldn't last because "people will soon get tired of staring at a plywood box every night." Even Thomas Watson, then the chairman of IBM, estimated in 1943 that there was a global market for a total of around five computers. It's easy to shake our heads at these statements now. But conventional wisdom is powerful, particularly when parroted by "experts" or people who often pretend to be experts.

We love to oversimplify life. Aphorisms abound. They're handed down through generations like heirlooms, time-tested tenets of truth. We circulate them on social media, readily pinning and retweeting, and invoke them in casual conversation and professional contexts alike. Some are sweet and (mostly) harmless. Others cement our mental paradigm and induce limited and destructive beliefs about our worldview and identity.

The problem with conventional wisdom is that it's generally lacking in nuance, an otherwise key component of life. Take the phrase "Money can't buy happiness." There are certainly some significant arguments in favor of this assertion. (Money itself can't comfort you when you're down or make you laugh.) But few would claim that money doesn't make life easier—it diminishes stress and gives you the opportunity to focus on things that *will* make you happy. So indirectly, yes, some money does buy a great deal of happiness.

Or take the popular parental cheer, "You can be anything you want when you grow up!" Of course the big caveat here is you can be anything you want IF you work hard, develop the skills, and have (or create) the resources to support that pursuit.

Finally, there's my personal favorite, "Just be yourself." That line, kindly intended to liberate and comfort, is confusing at best and disastrous at worst. We all have many sides to our personalities, and operating without a filter in all situations, simply in the name of "being you," often doesn't end well.

Conventional wisdom, then, is often not so wise.

And yet, once we're fed these platitudes—usually in impressionable childhood—they dictate how we understand our role and limitations (or lack thereof). We're too often quick to justify decisions with, "Well, it worked for my parents," or "But I've always . . ."—which isn't too far from what BlackBerry and Blockbuster unofficially said. And we've seen how well that worked out.

So why does all this misguided "wisdom" stick?

While companies have business models to guide and structure them, individuals have *mental models*. Psychologists believe we mentally create a version of reality from both knowledge and imagination, mixed in with our own individual perception. We then behave in a particular way as a result of the social and cultural structures crafted from this unique reality. Mental models not only construct reality, they help us mediate and navigate the world that confronts us each day. Our mental models start forming at birth and touch on everything from love to family to work to spirituality to politics.

Mental models allow our brains to go on autopilot. Take driving, for instance. Because of mental models, you're able to safely navigate the road for long distances, following all (or most) of the rules without actively thinking about them. Even when applied to a nonphysical task, mental models orient us to how the world operates and how to succeed in that system. And that conception of reality helps us rationalize future actions and beliefs.

So what's the problem with mental models? For one, they can induce irrational biases—we are predisposed to thinking and believing whatever reinforces our particular mental models. We frame things differently and therefore judge differently thanks to our mental models. They can also be oversimplified, misapplied, incomplete, or just flat out wrong. *Who could possibly want a telephone or a computer?* That statement was uttered as a result of mental models that became mental ruts, which are difficult to see beyond or dig yourself out of and thereby prohibit growth or evolved thinking. Sometimes people with conflicting mental models work against each other, which can fuel miscommunication and induce stagnancy or create behavior patterns that limit and restrict us.

Since the world is dynamic, not static, your mental state should follow suit. Always be aware of the mental models that might be holding you back and seek to look critically at every situation. Remember, there will always be a Netflix nipping at your heels, and you'll need to be flexible enough to stay competitive.

Irrational bias can grow out of some of the mental models we unconsciously rely on. This bias can in turn erode our capacity for empathy—a principle that underpins all civility and humanity and yet is sorely lacking from much of our current cultural and political discourse, not to mention the average personal exchange.

As a sociologist, one of the key tools I use in my research is fieldwork. This often involves one-on-one personal interviews. The goal of these conversations is not to trip up the person I'm interviewing or coax them into a particular perspective. Rather, I want them to open up, to speak with me like they would a close friend or family member—someone with whom they have years of history and established trust. And yet, when we sit down for the interview, it's often the first time we're meeting.

I do as much as I can to control the external elements: I minimize outside distractions, interruptions, and ambient noise and choose a familiar and comfortable location. We feel safe and comfortable around people who look like us, so I deliberately dress in a way that is relatable to my participants to disarm the conversation—something that won't offend or distract and that establishes a visual kinship—without looking like I'm mimicking them. I also try to be as present as possible, placing a discrete audio recorder on the table and taking minimal notes, which allows me to be fully engaged and make regular eye contact. But even with all this conscientious effort, sometimes there's a complete disconnect when we talk.

The X factor in the success or failure of these interviews is empathy—something that might sound obvious or easy, but which our mental models challenge. During one round of interviews, I spoke with female socialites. These were all women of extreme privilege—multiple homes, designer everything, professional portraits of their dogs on the walls. I simply couldn't relate. I'd convinced myself that we were diametrically opposed human beings. That our worldviews and perspectives were so disparate that I would immediately dislike them, and therefore the interviews would be worthless. But I knew that disliking them wasn't an option. I had to take that attitude off the table entirely. I could recognize all the many points of difference, but I had to forget about them. More importantly, I had to make my subjects forget. Because chances are, they weren't particularly keen on me, either. But it was my job to win them over.

We'd start off a little rough. They'd almost always begin by establishing a sense of urgency—some appointment they needed to run off to shortly. Most of their initial responses felt robotic: the sort of prescribed answers they'd given over and over. The kind of response you'd give a stranger. And then, without fail, somewhere during the first (painful) fifteen minutes or so, something would click. One of us would say something that the other could genuinely relate to—something that clearly mattered to both of us. Perhaps it was a relationship to a particular geographic location, like Nantucket or a recently closed West Village bar, or maybe it was something more abstract or even seemingly trivial—a perspective we both shared on why we never got manicures, a tactical strategy for getting across town quickly during rush hour, or a theory on why men in NYC wait so long to settle down (a topic that could hijack the conversation entirely). Whatever it was, it always arrived, eventually. And when it did, everything changed. The floodgates opened, and the interview began to flow freely. We became two old friends catching up, and the time crunch magically disappeared. A single point of connection—even a superficial one—shifted our mindset and single-handedly invalidated all the assumptions that were separating us. It shaped the rest of the conversation. That's not to say we all became best friends, but

I left every interview with rich material and a genuine respect and appreciation for the other person.

They were exactly the same people they had been when they walked in. As was I, of course. But our perception of each other had shifted. Our mental models were disrupted and recalibrated. So while these assumptions are often problematic, they also are mutable.

When they're working for us, these mental paradigms help us solve problems, communicate, interpret, and simplify situations so we can comprehend them and not get overwhelmed. But if your mental model is inaccurate or outdated, it can lead to negative or even catastrophic consequences. And if you think these paradigms only affect our own individual lives, you need look no further than the 2008 financial crisis, perhaps the most glaring recent example of the destructive capabilities of rampant assumptions. While a few prominent thinkers tried to warn of the impending collapse, the prevailing models blinded the financial authorities and the general populace alike. We were on a sinking boat, but the smoke machine from the floating party intoxicated most of us to the point of blindness.

Mental models also affect how we reflect on our actions. As a result of the economic crash and the subsequent recession, some individuals recalibrated their notions of "safety" and reprioritized their lives, opening the door to entrepreneurial living and thinking, something they had previously feared. Neuroplasticity is a real thing, and challenging and reformatting our mental models, while difficult, not only helps avoid future crises but also reveals a path to new, previously unforeseen opportunities.

Unlearning: we could all use a bit more of it. We spend so much time obsessed with acquiring new knowledge that we don't realize that a lot of not-so-useful knowledge—the inherited perspectives that box us in and weigh us down—also seeps in. It's time to break free from the shackles of groupthink and test these personal assumptions to see, once and for all, if they hold up. What are you taking for granted? What if you hit pause on acquiring knowledge and spent some time unlearning? What new paths or epiphanies might that offer you? Opportunity often knocks when we nudge ourselves from the limiting complacency of a default mind-set.

So how can we actively rebuke conventional wisdom and invalidate our assumptions?

One of my favorite examples of a startup that bucked the status quo and challenged the industry wisdom is the digital classifieds giant, Craigslist. Craig Newmark, the site's founder, changed the way we find a job, move, sell old furniture, and even date—all things that, before 1995, we looked for in print classified ads. What started as an events-based email list for friends grew to become one of the top job sites and one of the most heavily trafficked websites in the world. It was born of Newmark's desire to use technology to help people help each other, in the most direct way possible.

Since individuals self-publish and manage their own ads, Newmark eliminated the need for business development and sales. For anyone who's ever visited the site, it's obvious that flashy design is not a priority, but consumers don't seem to care. Craigslist works with and for the public, and no one else. (Need to find that beautiful girl you saw on the A train? No problem, head to the "Missed Connections" section and post an ad for her.) It's the people who power the site who have collectively saved billions of dollars in classified ads over the years. And even as Craigslist disrupted an industry, it simultaneously preserved its MVP mind-set, maintaining low-tech operations and repeatedly dragging us back to an era of one-on-one, email-driven transactions—because sometimes simplification is the most innovative action of all.

Disruption. It's one of Silicon Valley's favorite terms. Tech-Crunch, the popular technology news site, even hosts an annual conference called Disrupt. Entire industries—hospitality, music, publishing—have found their models disrupted by innovative startups rethinking those dusty paradigms. And while you don't have to create a new Craigslist, challenging the conventional wisdom and mental models you previously took for granted will positively disrupt your current trajectory, delivering more previously unforeseen opportunities and fewer missed connections.

SCRUM MASTER CHEAT SHEET

We can never escape all of the conventional wisdom that colors our perspective, but here are a few tricks to give even the most deeply ingrained personal paradigms a competitive refresh.

☛ **LOSE SIGHT OF DRY LAND.** A semester in Rome. A summer in Istanbul. Backpacking through Southeast Asia. Post-college, most adults find few opportunities for these sorts of immersive cultural exchanges beyond an annual weeklong vacation. But for many, it's those life-altering experiences that not only inform their worldviews but disrupt them. So what happens after we graduate? How do we continue to find such assumption-inverting opportunities? Taking a sabbatical from your life isn't always practical (or desirable), so we're left to draw from the increasingly distant memories of those powerful experiences or sink back into the habitual ease of the conventional wisdom that surrounds us. Neither of which is particularly satisfying or inspiring. So when we can't quit or flee, what's a viable alternative?

Startups operate in a comfort-free zone when they launch. Nearly everything is foreign, simply because it hasn't been done before, at least not in that particular way. And conventional wisdom quickly falls to the wayside, because it's the very thing they're innovating against. Everything is new, which brings not only a heart-stopping wave of vulnerability but also a liberating sense of wonder. Fresh eyes and a clean slate. The reason we talked so much about being open to (smart) risk in the previous chapters is because such openness disarms you and helps you escape the confines of your mental models. Once you've warmed to calculated risk, find ways to repeatedly broaden your horizons. From the culture you consume to the company you keep, most opportunities for stepping outside your comfort zone don't require a passport. Put yourself in situations that force you to engage with individuals outside of your usual groups—perhaps you'll work as a volunteer or mentor, or maybe you'll sign up for a language course or wander into an international market in your area. Public radio, podcasts, and documentaries about interesting topics can offer a direct path toward assumption inversion.

Author John Shedd wrote that "a ship in harbor is safe, but that is not what ships are made for."[5] By regularly losing sight of dry land through "foreign" encounters, no matter how close to home, you remove a perspective-binding safety net and accumulate experiences that push the boundaries of your sense of self and purpose—of how you live and what is possible. It's the difference between active and passive living. Pull up your anchor regularly, even if you don't physically stray too far.

☞ **CHECK YOUR VISION.** Humans are naturally resistant to change. Accepting change is our life medicine, and we often come to it kicking and screaming. As we strive to challenge our current assumptions, we need both a willingness to let go *and* the ability to adjust our vision. Rethinking how you view something or how something gets done may seem small and insignificant, but it may lead to a larger shift in perspective, actions, and outcomes—a sort of paradigm shift domino effect. All the micro-experiments you conduct allow you to defog your assumption goggles and build new mental models. To avoid groupthink, force yourself to examine how you reached any given conclusion and ask others to do the same (whenever appropriate) in a casual "Hey, that's interesting. What led you to that?" kind of way. Encouraging an articulated explanation from both yourself and others helps to sniff out any default mental models driving the decisions or perspectives and messing with the outcome. That's not to say you can always control the outcome of that particular situation in the moment, but you will create a more fertile foundation for transparency and clarity.

☞ **UPDATE YOUR SOFTWARE.** Technology, like mental models, is only cutting-edge for so long. Even the most groundbreaking new inventions eventually expire and become outdated. But aside from a cracked screen or a phone in the toilet, it can be difficult to know when it's time to trade up. Unfortunately, a trip to the Genius Bar won't cut it when it comes to our mental system upgrades.

Our troubleshooting protocol begins with a close examination of what ideas are waning. *Which assumptions are no longer valid? Which mental models are past their prime or should be retired to the archives of your life?* Too often we don't ask these questions or interrogate our mode of existence until crisis strikes: it usually takes one devastating computer crash to force you to consistently backup your work. So do an initial large-scale interrogation of each major facet of your life (chances are, most of them are related), then make a habit of hitting pause to scan for any necessary updates on a regular basis.

And don't forget: upgrades demand a network connection. You'll need to rely on those around you to help you make changes to your mental paradigms. As you stay immersed in your social or work group, make sure that you are not dodging self-reflection and breakthroughs in order to avoid conflict with your peers. Additionally, as you begin challenging group norms, you may want to tread lightly. It's great to be an early adopter, but challenging assumptions can seem threatening to the group, so roll out the mental revisions gradually.

THE LAZY LOWDOWN: TOP TEN CHAPTER TAKEAWAYS

1. Conventional wisdom is often not so wise.
2. Don't be a BlackBerry; innovate before it's too late.
3. Resist the casual complacency of groupthink.
4. Mental models make our worlds go round, but sometimes in the wrong direction.
5. Embrace empathy and feel others' pain; keep irrational biases at bay.
6. Be the Netflix that takes down slow-moving competition.
7. Disruption awakens sleeping giants, so make mindful changes.
8. Keep "missed connections" voyeuristically romantic, not laced with regret.
9. Cast your experiential net wide—or better yet, ditch the net and swim toward discomfort.
10. Today is the perfect day to unlearn.

5.

Win Every Room

Efficiency is doing things right; effectiveness is doing the right things.

—Peter F. Drucker, *The Effective Executive: The Definitive Guide to Getting the Right Things Done*

Mickey came from humble beginnings. Raised in a one-bedroom apartment in the Bronx, he was the first in his family to go to college. After finding his professional footing in business school, he started working in fashion retail, quickly climbing the ranks to the position of buyer at large department stores like Bloomingdale's and Macy's, and finally to CEO: first at Ann Taylor, then the Gap, and finally J.Crew.[1]

A master transformer, Mickey knew how to take a flailing company and catapult it to the top. Twenty-five years after the Gap first launched, and following a prolonged dip when trendier retailers outpaced it, the brand was reborn to prominence under his watch. It not only reclaimed its status as the go-to spot for fashion basics, but it helped shape the cultural landscape of the 1990s with its clever advertising campaigns. Mickey redefined affordable American style and made mundane staples like khakis and t-shirts desirable. And while he gave the Gap a new "casual chic" image, he also boosted sales at its sister store, Banana Republic, and launched its spinoff discount chain, Old Navy. That winning streak eventually ended, and in 2002 he was suddenly and unceremoniously ousted from the company he'd saved. Never down for long, Mickey was immediately scooped up by another 25-year-old iconic American brand, J.Crew, where he once again worked his magic.

In recent years, however, J.Crew has fallen on hard times, which critics largely attribute to a shift from classic basics to overpriced, impractical pieces of diminishing quality. In 2015, sales dropped and J.Crew fired 10 percent of its employees.[2] But while the companies he's led have experienced some ups and downs, Mickey's legacy as the "Merchant Prince" remains. His success can't be attributed to mere creative genius or a flair for fashion; it's his (stylish) boots-on-the-ground commitment to constant innovation that drives his achievements. He still makes surprise visits to stores, where he engages employees and customers, brainstorming with them how to make the experience better.[3] He questions everything from the music to a singular product's placement, responding to customers who email him at his publicly available address by calling them directly or inviting them to team meetings.[4] If you meet him, he'll likely poll your purchasing behavior, probing for what you've bought, why, and how you liked it. There's no unimportant store; Mickey's philosophy is that all the small pieces add up to something big.

Successful innovation comes from obsessing over details—not simply focusing on top-line revenue and long-term vision. Millard

"Mickey" Drexler operates like an entrepreneur even as he helms some of the world's largest corporations. And he's obsessed with his customers. He understands that success is determined less by the execution of his personal preferences than by his ability to interpret and deliver what the customer wants.

This seemingly clairvoyant ability to predict human desire—and then deliver it—is akin to what the startup world refers to as "product-market fit." Once a product meets the needs of its target market—and at a profit—it reaches product-market fit and can begin scaling, a term startups use for profitable growth and expansion. But this is no easy feat. Startup founders often underestimate the time it will take to validate their product and market; it's not unusual for it to take two to three times longer than anticipated.

Remember the MVP "beta" mode I mentioned? It's the early stage of product development, where bugs abound and kinks are constant. Well, on the road to establishing product-market fit, companies often cling to the beta label—even companies that might seem like they're all polish, all the time, like Google.

Gmail was created as a Google side project back in 2001. It became the internal email system of Google, and two and a half years later, in April 2004, it launched publicly—but not without controversy. Gmail created a sort of identity crisis for Google. Their core offering was Search, not email. Were they just getting distracted? Should they stick to what they knew? In addition to the question of whether Gmail was "Google" enough, there were technical hurdles. To create the features they desired, the coders needed to write in JavaScript, a coding language that had failed in the past and seemed risky because of its tendency to crash. But JavaScript code worked directly on a user's computer, making it exponentially faster in its responsiveness than the more widespread HTML (which required a page refresh for updates), so they found a way to make it work.

When Gmail was publicly released, Google labeled it "beta" and only offered access to 1,000 people—making it an exclusive rollout. Key industry influencers were invited in an effort to grow incrementally while gaining strategic feedback. The limited release was a clever marketing tactic that created interest and demand, and also allowed Google to refine the product. Part of what made Gmail more attractive than other email servers was its user experience, which reimagined email as clusters of "conversations," as well as the large storage capabilities, which allowed users to keep their emails forever without running out of space. Despite its popularity, Gmail remained in beta mode for five years—and eventually became the industry standard in email. By 2015, Gmail reached 900 million users,[5] far outpacing Yahoo Mail and Hotmail. Staying in beta for a prolonged period allowed Gmail to remain experimental, grow its loyal user base, refine its features, and expand its server capacity over time.

On the flip side, the companies Mickey Drexler led were long past their beta stage and were experiencing slumps that forced them to reevaluate. He constantly reconfigured each company's product-market fit, even decades after it first launched. The lesson? Even when you think you've "got it right," you may need to start over at any time. Because the market—like life—is fluid.

So what does product-market fit have to do with your life?

You don't need to be launching a startup or running a Fortune 500 company to benefit from understanding your audience's needs. Nothing and no one operates in isolation, and you can't establish product-market fit without knowing your audience well. Whether we're pushing out a product or we *are* the product, we are social creatures, and our actions demand validation from those around us. As you try to find your niche—whether it's personal or professional—staying nimble and picking up on contextual clues is key. And there's no context too mundane for analysis.

What is your "market" demanding? Is anyone buying what you're selling? From the dating market to the job market, catering to your audience is not about selling out or losing your sense of self to appeal to the masses—it's about finding the overlaps between what's true to you and what resonates with them. That's your sweet spot.

In 1886, David McConnell was a traveling book salesman when he observed that his homemade perfume—something he had initially offered as a "free gift with purchase"—was more popular than his books. So using the same door-to-door model, McConnell pivoted his product offering, with one key difference: he recruited women to sell to other women. The women related best to one another, and since there were few opportunities for women to work outside the home, door-to-door sales complemented their existing lifestyle while giving them some extra money. It was a home run. McConnell went on to create a perfume company and recruit sales reps—of which there are still six million worldwide. Eventually, the company expanded into a full line of cosmetics under the name Avon.[6] (So yes, the first "Avon lady" was a man.)

Around the same time that David McConnell was giving away perfume samples, William Wrigley Jr. was selling his family soap and giving away baking powder as the free gift. And like McConnell, Wrigley soon realized that his free gift—the baking powder—was far more popular than the soap itself. So he started selling the baking powder and threw in some chewing gum with every purchase. Yet again, Wrigley realized that his free gift was more popular than what he sold. So he abandoned the soap and the baking powder and developed a line of chewing gum under his name. Not only a savvy entrepreneur but also an advertising pioneer, William Wrigley Jr. created the first nationwide direct mail marketing campaign: he sent gum to every single person in the phone book, from coast to coast.[7]

William Wrigley Jr. said, "Anyone can make gum. The trick is to sell it."[8] Good ideas abound, but the ability to follow through is where you start to separate from the pack. We often start projects but fail to complete them, not because they're too hard, but because they're not fun. But there are ways to make onerous tasks enjoyable. We think games are either for children or digital gamers, when in reality, gamifying your life makes many less-than-entertaining situations opportunities for fun. Games are more than just silly outlets. They motivate us to achieve goals and develop better behaviors and habits, and they also build social bonds and help us invest in our networks. Games are largely not motivating because of some big final payout—sometimes referred to as an extrinsic reward. Rather, they compel us to keep going with the promise of intrinsic rewards, which are intangible, internal, and often rooted in emotion. While they surprise, delight, and amuse us, games also reward us with prosocial emotions like love, compassion, admiration, and devotion—all of which foster lasting happiness. The promise of positive emotional infusions along the strenuous journey to success changes the game entirely—and makes selling "it" (whatever that may be) both easier and more fun.

That's not to say that one's gaze should be turned entirely internally. Both Wrigley and McConnell understood their customers and knew not only how to create a product that appealed to them—and how to stay motivated in the process—but also how to deliver it in a desirable way.

And that brings us to the second key point of product-market fit: delivery. Mickey Drexler doesn't just analyze his merchandise; he obsesses over every aspect of it, especially the point at which the merchandise and the customer meet. Perhaps no one understands the importance of this interface better than Tony Hsieh.

Zappos sells shoes. And clothing. A lot of it. But that's not all they're known for. If you ask CEO Tony Hsieh what he sells, customer service is likely at the top of his list. Zappos is a company built on customer feedback and satisfaction. And customers seem to be very satisfied: nearly 75 percent are repeat buyers.[9]

In 2000, only a year after it launched, Zappos brought in $1.6 million in revenue. The next year, revenue rose to $8.6 million. By 2008, the company hit $1 billion in sales.[10] Could any shoes be so extraordinary? Why did customers keep coming back for more? It wasn't the wares; it was the entire shopping experience. Sure, Zappos offers free shipping and free returns, but Hsieh takes it a step further and makes a positive experience part of the company culture: he created ten core company values and makes a practice of only hiring employees who share those values.[11] He then does something many managers are too insecure to do: he gives employees "permission"—that is to say, he empowers his employees to make decisions and "be themselves." They don't work off of a script when speaking with customers or corresponding with them on email. They stay on the line and communicate with customers until their needs are met (legend has it that one call lasted over ten hours[12]). Hsieh markets Zappos through a commitment to truly exceptional customer service. He believes that talking to someone on the phone for five to ten minutes—if the experience is positive—creates an enduring memory amongst the customers, and they're likely to spread the word to friends. One rep sent a loyal client flowers after she forgot to return some shoes due to a death in the family.[13] Another time, UPS mistakenly rerouted a man's shoes and, unwilling to let him go barefoot to a wedding in which he was best man, a rep overnighted him free shoes.[14] Needless to say, these individuals became customers for life. Over the years, Zappos repeatedly prioritized humanity over immediate profits—clearly without sacrificing the latter.

Hsieh and his team at Zappos "deliver happiness" (as his bestselling book reminds us[15]) not only to customers but also to his

employees. After an initial training period, Hsieh offers new re-
cruits a $2,000 bonus to quit on the spot[16]—an attempt to weed out
the people just looking for cash and not interested in being part of
the Zappos corporate family (one of their core values). And given
their stellar performance, Hsieh and Zappos have proven that
happiness—for both customers and employees—can be profitable.

A perpetual innovator, Hsieh's latest move is perhaps his
most radical: he did away with all manager positions and job ti-
tles at Zappos—a system known as holacracy—and bet on self-
organization as the more effective tool for success.[17] To ensure
that everyone was on board with the transition, Hsieh offered a
severance package to employees if they didn't like the direction in
which the company was moving (14 percent took it[18]). While the
merits and sustainability of this organizational experiment are
still being tested—and early reports indicate it's still confusing for
the employees[19]—its principles are clear: empowering employees
to self-govern and practice autonomy allows them to think and
operate like entrepreneurs while still within the corporate walls.

Hsieh is driven not by the products he sells, but by the way his
company makes his employees and customers feel. And it's that
feeling that spreads virally in the mythic stories about how great
it is to work at Zappos, or about how stellar their customer service
is. Most employees don't sing the praises of their employer, and
when's the last time you swooned over a customer service interaction? It takes something remarkably different to drive that level of
engagement in today's fragmented world.

Zappos's success demonstrates that companies are measured
as much by the way they do business as the quality of what they
sell. And we are no different. After the final bell of high school,
where reputation is everything, it's easy to forget that interpersonal skills matter as much as the goods we deliver. So what's
your personal company culture? We spend so much time obsessing

over *what* we'll do with our lives that we often fail to invest in *how* we'll do it. How do you live your life? How do you treat not only others but yourself? What rules govern how you operate? It's the accumulation of these microdecisions around the way you self-govern that determines your reputation—and your reputation is a valuable currency. It's not just the work we produce or the tasks we complete. It's also the way we travel from A to B. How do you show up? And what's your strategy for connecting with people once you're there? Happily, you don't have to leave that connection to chance.

Startups sometimes use a methodology called "design thinking" when trying to understand their audience's needs and establish product-market fit. Originally used in the design and product development communities, design thinking now shakes up problem solving in all areas of business and life.

Take Ikea. It doesn't just design furniture; it also innovates the way a furniture company operates and the way consumers engage with its products and stores. From self-assembly to flat packaging, Ikea redesigned the furniture acquisition experience for the masses—what the company calls "democratic design."[20] Their business model and their product design strategy are aligned. And they aren't just thinking about the furniture: Ikea designs the entire shopping experience of its customers. Food markets and a children's playground cater to the whole family and the whole body—some customers go just for the Swedish meatballs. Ikea even partnered with Marriott to launch Moxy, a hotel chain aimed specifically at Millennials—a user base to which Ikea's emphasis on stylish affordability appeals. (If only they could apply a little more design thinking to their madness-inducing assembly instructions.)

In the design thinking mind-set, you are looking to understand someone else's point of view rather than just impose your own. How? You immerse yourself in your audience's personal contexts and observe—you get inside their heads and develop a deep understanding of them. While in their shoes, you discover their unmet needs, which inform the solutions you offer. Design thinking asks you to think beyond the new and cool and consider the unpopular, even the once unthinkable.

After college, I joined the Peace Corps. I had a very idealistic vision of how my service would change the world (I was 22, after all). I was assigned to an economically impoverished community in the Dominican Republic. Electricity and water were intermittent, and advanced education and exposure to the arts were luxuries reserved for the wealthy.

My official assignment was to teach farmers to run their farms like businesses by taking out loans—not really my area of expertise, but one I was willing to try. So with little to no relevant training, I went through the motions and organized meetings to rally the community. But no one came. And the few who did show up, hours late, seemed far more interested in seeing their neighbors and eating the free snacks than listening to what I had to say. Something was off.

Meanwhile, not far from the home I was renting, there was a little zinc-roofed wooden shack that housed the local "music school." Every day, children and young adults would come to the one-room schoolhouse to play half-broken, donated instruments. But the scene wasn't just quaint, it was shocking: the music, by any standards, was incredible. The sounds they produced using tattered tools and low-wage instruction was alive and exuberant in an otherwise desolate environment. I knew I had to get involved.

The school also housed a donated piano, but no one knew how to play it. I'd played for years and briefly taught lessons in high school, so I told the director to send me a few of the students, thinking I'd teach two or three in my spare time (which was plentiful—

my official assignment occupied only a few hours of my week. And there was no Internet.) Over 20 students showed up—on time—to the first meeting, with more students begging to be let in. We established weekly lesson times, and I solicited sheet music from my former instructor in the United States and keyboard donations from wealthy local expats. The students not only never missed a lesson, they practiced on their keyboards for several hours each day (sometimes without electricity and therefore without sound).

Extended families and neighbors spilled out of the tiny space during our regular concert series. I raised money and started a scholarship fund for a few of the truly exceptional students to study at the music conservatory several hours away—requiring them to come back and serve as music educators in their hometown to repay their debt and pass on the gift. The program anchored the students' lives and became a point of great pride as it evolved into a permanent fixture in the community.

And yet, my proposal for the arts education program was rejected by the Peace Corps and received no support—they actually threatened to kick me out if I kept pursuing it, but I (scandalously) ignored their warnings. It was easy to say there were other, more basic, unmet needs, and therefore creative endeavors would be mere frivolity in an atmosphere of austerity. But the students didn't just pick up a useless hobby. They developed a skill and honed a craft and, with it, gained the "soft" skills that accompany that sort of focused engagement: respect and responsibility, and commitment and discipline. These invaluable attributes and lessons came to permeate their lives and their vision of themselves. Arts education ignited their imaginations and allowed them to see themselves and the world they inhabited differently. Playing music wasn't just something they did; it shaped who they were.

The best way for me to excel and serve my audience wasn't to impose what the Peace Corps thought they needed or what had been politically pre-negotiated. And what the community wanted—what all people want, regardless of their situation—went way beyond the survival "basics." It was the intersection of my talents and the community's demands and interests that helped me find product-market fit and best serve my community. And that took more than planning and spreadsheets. It meant on-the-ground observations and one-on-one interactions. It was a real-time endeavor, laced with uncertainty but surging with promise.

Remember that many of the biggest innovations seemed impossible, or at least impractical, at first. Often, our most rewarding experiences and accomplishments seemed similarly foolish at conception. But once you tap into the brains and hearts of your audience—and locate the part of you that resonates—the right fit isn't too far behind.

SCRUM MASTER CHEAT SHEET

Appealing to your audience is a lifelong pursuit. And since intuition has its limits, it pays to invest in a little mindfulness to deepen your connections and elevate your market value. Here's how to become a hotter commodity and increase the value of both your social stock and your happiness portfolio.

☞ **PRACTICE RADICAL EMPATHY.** Game-changing epiphanies and valuable insights are rarely obvious or straightforward. They often emerge from the nuances. Embrace a design thinking mindset and approach each problem and context through the lens of your audience. Design thinking focuses on desired outcomes and unmet needs (which are usually unarticulated and must be intuited). Dive headfirst into real-world experience and human interaction to understand what your audience values—

which is more illuminating than simply asking them what they want. This human-centric approach demands that you ask yourself: Did you leave a lingering impression on your audience? How did you make them feel? Many times, *how* you interact is as important as what you ultimately deliver. It's not just about the final product, it's also about what happens along the way—all of which contributes to how you're perceived (something we'll delve into in the next chapter). This may all sound a bit Machiavellian; is empathy and human-centeredness really just a covert power play? Consider the alternative: operating without empathy or in a way that does not appeal to or please your audience does not leave anyone feeling great. Any tactic can be used for evil, but investing your time and energy in operating from an empathic perspective does more than help you win the room—it makes your audience feel like winners, too.

☞ GAMIFY YOUR LIFE. Begin by defining your competitive advantage. What do you want when you walk into your office? What's your objective at that party? We all want something in each setting. It may be material or monetary, or maybe it's just an emotion we're chasing. Whatever it is, make it a game. Not to cheapen it, but because games are fun. And they motivate us—both internally and externally. I'm not suggesting you hold yourself to an impossible standard in every situation. Nor is it useful to actively compete with everyone around you. But that doesn't mean you can't set a goal and actively pursue it. You can gamify any aspect of your life: productivity, fitness, fiscal responsibility, or social participation. From private tracking apps to social check-ins, even the most grueling of tasks can receive a fun infusion. Or if you're not tech savvy and want more nondigital options, remember that game mechanics can be applied with or without Wi-Fi. Clearly define your goal, whether it's a savings target or a fitness objective, then set metrics and develop a reward system—perhaps you accumulate points to "unlock" a splurge at each new level. You need some sort of payoff, even though the flood of intrinsic rewards also keeps you motivated along the journey. You're the game designer, and whatever pushes you to level up is a win. Choose to be a competitor, even if only against yourself.

☛ **UP YOUR STREET CRED**. A company's marketplace reputation is a huge factor in its ongoing success. And while you may not be peddling a product, your credibility matters. But it's not something you buy or acquire instantly—there's no street cred app. It's earned over time, often through triumph over hardship, not impeccability. It's exhibited through consistent loyalty and walking the walk. It's a combination of skills and experiences, and ongoing social proof—where your audience witnesses others investing in or validating your actions and ideas—is key to establishing legitimacy. Like the Zappos rep who stays on the telephone troubleshooting for hours or goes the extra mile to deliver the perfect shoes, your isolated acts can become the stuff of your own mythic reality. Everyday heroism—whether it's offering up a seat or staying present with a friend in need—fuels the word-of-mouth testimonials that cement who you are, not just what you can do.

THE LAZY LOWDOWN: TOP TEN CHAPTER TAKEAWAYS

1. Be the Merchant Prince of your own life.
2. Product-market fit demands lifelong vigilance. Don't get too comfortable.

3. The intersection of your audience's demand and what's true to you is your sweet spot.

4. Sometimes the free gift with purchase is the surprise winner—so pay attention to the periphery.

5. It's not just what you do, it's how you make people feel along the way.

6. Become a designer (if only in your mind).

7. Your personal company culture matters.

8. Deliver more than the basics. Mere surviving is not thriving.

9. Life is a game. Be a competitor.

10. You rep is your currency. Cash in.

6.

Work It

The greatest that man can achieve is his own appearance.
—HANNAH ARENDT, *The Human Condition*

Ralph was born in the Bronx to Ashkenazi Jewish parents. While still a teenager, he changed his last name from Lifshitz to Lauren, a symbolic predecessor of the persona he would soon create for himself. After two years, he dropped out of college and joined the army, which he then also dropped, trading in his fatigues for the equally distinctive but radically different Brooks Brothers uniform.[1]

One day after attending a polo match, something clicked in Ralph. It was the 1960s, a time when plain skinny neckties were all the rage, but he had a vision for a new high-end brand anchored in wide, colorful, European ties. He designed the ties and launched his own company, Polo, which later evolved into a full menswear line. Today, the brand that started with wide neckties encompasses everything you could possibly dream of wearing or living in: men's, women's, and children's clothing; home furnishings; scents—you can literally immerse yourself in the manufactured world of Ralph Lauren.

Ralph Lauren was one of the first apparel lines to branch out into more than clothes, and it does it spectacularly well. Beyond the ties and tailored threads, Ralph Lauren sells you a lifestyle: a high-class, polo-playing vision of yourself, surrounded by nothing but beauty and comfort. Ralph Lifshitz's name, his biography, his native culture—none of that mattered. If he could imagine and dream it, he could create and become it. Ralph drew his inspiration not from his own unglamorous New York existence, but from the movies and WASP-y stars who delighted him[2]: Cary Grant, Fred Astaire, blue-blooded Americana, Hollywood glamour, effortless preppiness. And in the end, none of his life circumstances kept him from achieving that goal. Reality resided in his imagination, and fantasy fueled the persona he was creating—not only for himself, but for millions of consumers.

Ralph is famously quoted as saying, "I don't design clothes. I design dreams." And he was fittingly chosen as the designer for the 1974 film version of *The Great Gatsby*. After all, Ralph Lauren and Jay Gatsby are not so dissimilar. Gatsby also changed his name as a teenager—from Gatz to Gatsby—and grew up outside of the high society to which he aspired. They both dropped out of college, served in the military, have strong ties to New York, and are self-made success stories. But for both Ralph and Jay, their personas weren't just about the accumulation of wealth: they were about creating the appearance of belonging. They embody the power of transformation and the promise that strategically con-structed appearances can trump birthright—at least in America.

But are they "authentic"? We throw that word around a lot these days. But what does it really mean? What constitutes au-thenticity? Why should we seek it? And might the pursuit of it actually undermine what might really make us happy?

Some might call him a poser, but Ralph Lauren exemplifies a radical reformulation of authenticity. He not only launched a com-pany, he created an entirely new identity. His very sense of self, as well as the world's perception of him, sprang from his company. His industry domination sprang from the actualization of his *possible* self, not his biographical self. Ralph Lauren's daring life suggests that appearances *are* authentic. Creating and living our desired reality *is* authentic. You don't have to rethink your identity as radically as Ralph did, but your image is yours for the making.

We are all actors in our own lives. Our identities move fluidly between the face meant for public viewing—our polished perso-nas where we're (at least somewhat) ready for our close-ups—and the preparatory realm, where we're not quite ready for primetime—what I like to call our "rollers in the hair" stage. Ideally, we want to control public access to the preparatory realm. But thanks in part to technology and social media (something we'll explore in the next chapter), that isn't always possible.

So are we always acting in social settings? Can public behaviors ever be authentic? It's time to stop obsessing over authenticity—at least our old conception of it. The truth is, your front and back stages are, in a sense, both affectations. Even when you're at home alone looking at yourself in the mirror, your assessment of your reflection is informed by the potential future judgment of others. Our private selves are as socially constructed as our pub-lic personas.

Our fashion choices are equally problematic when held to the standard of authenticity. We claim we want to "dress for ourselves," as if that's an absolute categorization unsusceptible to change or influence. And pleasing ourselves doesn't fully encompass why we opt for the little black dress over the yoga pants. We are witnessed creatures, and our appearances not only reflect and shape reality, they also assist us in the negotiation of social capital. You need audience buy-in.

Fashion historian Anne Hollander argues that we dress in a way to look "right," not fashionable.[3] We want to feel like we fit in more than we want to look like we just stepped off a runway. We crave sartorial product-market fit; we need it to feel comfortable. And sometimes feeling "right" means moving beyond the confines of your biographical circumstances toward your possible self.

A/B testing is a startup tactic that involves the strategic comparison of two variables in an effort to gauge which performs better. Applying this methodology to how you self-present allows you to physically embody the limitless experimentality of being, not settle for the confines of a predetermined narrative. That's not to say our true biographies are inconsequential. To the contrary, they anchor and guide our explorations of who we might become. It's the combination of the two—the life you've lived and the one you've imagined—that, once visually articulated and tangibly manifested, has the power to resonate most potently.

Power. It's not just the realm of a billionaire founder or an elected official. The micro-circumstances of our everyday lives are all laced with power dynamics. From jockeying for a place in line to formal job interviews, we are constantly granted or stripped of power, to varying degrees. We often want to believe that the negotiation of power stems from merit, hard work, and intellectual substance. But one other key factor has the power to crush or catapult those efforts: appearance. It may seem superficial, but your appearance is powerful. The visual symbols you present demonstrate everything from socioeconomic status to subculture affiliation—all of which facilitates the negotiation of power. Yes, there's more to you than meets the eye, but that visual snapshot frames everything else.

Like it or not, we cannot avoid fashion. It permeates all facets of the social world: our individual affinities and professional affiliations, the technology that mediates our vision of others and ourselves, and the landscape of our commodified bodies and branded identities. In each case, we consciously and subconsciously dress and groom ourselves in an effort to convey that we are relevant and in-demand.

Some refuse to submit and take an "anti-fashion" or image-agnostic stance to personal appearance. They erroneously believe they're exempt from visual communication because they shun trends and avoid shopping as much as possible. But, protest though they may, we all participate in fashion: we make and reject particular looks every day. Whether you're in decades-old bargain-basement purchases or crisp khaki pants and a button-down, fashion neutral does not exist.

There is a difference, however, between opting out and being consciously consistent. Eliminating visual choice through the creation of a personal uniform can be liberating. Think of the self-appointed uniforms we so closely associate with some of our modern power players: Steve Jobs's black mock turtleneck, jeans, and New Balance sneakers; Marissa Mayer's bottomless couture closet; Barack Obama's predictable blue or gray power suits. The unofficial uniform you design for yourself displays a type of mask. These masks allow us to reveal or highlight different aspects of our identities. But sartorial masking is not about duplicity. It's a sort of information game we play with our audience, as people interact differently with us based on the masks we display.

Neither meaning nor power are intrinsic in any single article of clothing. Nor is anything inherently fashionable. The significance changes with the time and place, and it's important to always notice changing contexts and adjust our fashion accordingly. A failure to evolve can leave us visually misunderstood and left to operate from a position of weakness. Dress, like language, is complex, and there are no simple statements.

Once you've accepted the significance of your appearance, how do you optimize the way you look? Some say you can't buy taste, but can you strategically develop effective style?

In my twenties, I spent many summers living and working on Nantucket Island, a privileged playground for the uber-rich off the coast of Massachusetts. To call Nantucket preppy is a supreme understatement. It's all popped collars and neon colors, sockless loafers and headbands, ribbon belts and whale pants—and, of course, Ralph Lauren's signature Polo shirts (the ironic origins of which seemed lost on the towheaded WASPs—just as Ralph would want it).

While there, I worked at a small, high-end clothing boutique. The merchandise rarely went on sale, and the markup was extremely healthy. They carried primarily luxe fabrics, custom shearlings, and small, European designers—all of which made it a hot destination for the Nantucket elite. At times, I managed the store and assisted the owner in the seasonal buying of merchandise, but my primary function was simply to sell.

I remember the first time I walked into the store at age 21. I'd never been around such exquisite (or expensive) things. I did a double-take on the prices, certain there were accidental zeros. That first summer, when the owner was so short-staffed he literally got on his knees and begged me to come work for him, my style was anything but preppy. I wore a mostly black, piecemeal wardrobe comprised of international flea market finds and spandex dance clothes (it looked better than it sounds, I swear), accessorized with some type of chunky, colorful jewelry of varying ethnic origins—a stark contrast to the pearls and button-downs that surrounded me.

I'd always been fascinated by style and its transformative powers, so despite my sticker shock, I took the job. I quickly learned that the blindingly preppy paraphernalia that paraded in and out of the store was more than just fashion—it was a tool for my success in that space. Each customer displayed specific indicators of their membership in various social groups. My job was to quickly recognize the dress code presented to me and thereby serve the individual in the most effective manner (that is, get them to buy as much stuff as possible). Luxury designers and large diamond rings, coupled with any one of many "it bags," were indicators of The Elite. Patagonia or some other fleece-centric outdoor attire in muted colors, paired with practical footwear, pointed to The Locals. Backpacks, shopping bags from less expensive, more tourist-oriented shops, and a basic ensemble of khaki shorts, white sneakers, and a t-shirt with something along the lines of "I AM THE MAN FROM NANTUCKET" printed across it set off the Day-Tripper alert. But those were just the main categorizations—dozens of hierarchical subsets operated within each of them.

Not only did I study customers' aesthetic choices, I also used my new understanding of them to manipulate my own appearance. I hypothesized that if I could look like them, they would relate to me, and my sales would go up significantly. Gradually, I started testing out different pieces of the sartorial puzzle. I swapped out my all-black uniform for mostly white, acquired a few pastel polos (collars always popped), and traded my large, funky jewelry for teeny, tiny, diamond stud earrings. Same person, different image. It allowed me to use my own style as an example when working with the customers, giving us a basic starting point for building a connection. The hypothesis proved accurate, and my sales soared.

You've probably been in a situation like this—one in which you need to bridge the gap between yourself and your audience. Where the first impression you presented didn't line up with unwritten rules and expectations. This is yet another opportunity to observe, hypothesize, and test.

But in my quest to connect, did I become less "authentic"? Who cares? In situations like this, you need to fit in, even if you might want to stand out, or at least express some individuality. That's when it pays to practice what I call "distinguished compliance," in which obedience to the social norm is just as important as projecting your comfortable default. If your "authentic" appearance is at odds with the local aesthetic, it may be perceived as socially rebellious and alienating. A combination of personal distinction and a visual nod that you "get it" is the most successful recipe for facilitating connections. In the delicate balance between individuality and conformity, an extreme embrace of either is rarely the winning formula.

The good news is—no matter your preference or predicament—there isn't a single successful look, and confidence can overshadow many a sartorial flub. What is perceived as "visual correctness" in any given context is an ongoing, holistic operation, not a precise science.

Trying on visual identities allows you to gain a deeper understanding of yourself while providing an opportunity for individualized expression. Long after my Nantucket years, one method I've used for conducting research involves dressing up in personas far from my usual aesthetic. Over the course of one year, I dressed up in a series of archetypal outfits to test the boundaries of my own identity.

I began with a categorization I actively avoid: that of a tourist. I hate being a tourist. They are inherently clumsy in their attempts to negotiate public transportation, never seem to master the local aesthetic, and tend to champion the city's attractions that most urban residents avoid with disdain. But it's for these reasons that assuming the role of a New York City tourist excited me. It was my chance to wander in wide-eyed awe without so much as a hint of self-consciousness. I gave myself permission to be hopelessly un-hip and dressed accordingly: spandex biking shorts, sensible walking shoes, "I ♥ New York" t-shirt, a baseball cap with the Statue of Liberty stitched on, and, of course, the requisite fanny pack. As a tourist, my group affiliations were radically realigned. I interacted with individuals I encountered on a daily basis—souvenir shopkeepers, street musicians, the Times Square caricaturists—but whose attention normally bypassed me without my tourist gear. My visual transformation into a tourist redefined my place in the urban social strata, while my actual persona and biographical details remained the same. Perhaps the best part of being a tourist was the license to be deliciously oblivious to disapproving stares, wayward glances, and mocking comments. (If only we all had a little more tourist in us.)

In another experiment, I dressed as one might imagine a prostitute would: a tight, revealing mini-dress, a peek-out bra, hot pink fishnets, a bobbed wig with a distinct pink streak, and five-inch stilettos, complete with clear plastic platforms and rhinestone heels. Fully costumed, I felt sexy in a non-pretty sort of way—a type of gritty glamour one doesn't often experience in everyday life. The extreme shortness of the dress (which kept riding up in the back, demanding constant adjustment), coupled with half-exposed breasts and the most uncomfortable footwear I've ever worn, induced a feeling of perpetual physical self-consciousness and awkwardness. I felt unrecognizable, even to myself, which gave me the license to confidently embody a persona and physicality that might otherwise be judged as inappropriate. Observers were left to wonder if I was going to solicit them—not because I was actually selling my body, but because I was able to materialize that intent in a visually convincing manner.

Given my Iranian roots, I also used this series of experiments to try on the veil. I grew up with my blonde-haired, blue-eyed, Irish Catholic mother in the Midwest, but my father is Persian. Though many believe I most resemble my mother, my hair, eyes, and olive skin tone, along with the shape of my eyes and broad cheeks, give away my Middle Eastern heritage to knowing observers. Had I grown up in Iran, the veil would be part of my everyday existence. The veil is a garment that is frequently assumed to be a consequence of social and political oppression and a symbol of imposed modesty, which leaves little room for individuality and expression, let alone rebellion. And while I ultimately felt invisible, more reserved, and uncomfortably conservative in my veil, that is not a uniform response to wearing it—nor is its meaning and significance universal or inherent in the garment.

Finally, I stepped out of my normally highly feminine persona and assumed a more androgynous aesthetic. I wore roomy camouflage cargo pants with a silver chain hanging from the belt loops; a heavy-duty plain black t-shirt that hung loosely over my flattened chest; a black leather arm cuff; combat boots; a baseball cap with my hair tucked completely out of sight; thick, square-framed glasses; and a toothpick in my mouth. I no longer exuded femininity: my curves were hidden, my shoulders were hunched slightly, my hands were kept deep within my pockets. My androgynous attire allowed me to redefine attractiveness for myself while playing with the fluidity of both the male and female gaze.

My possible self became my real self during these experiments, however briefly. Playing with how you visually tell your story can be therapeutic and even shift the narrative of your life. The fluctuation in my social capital and self-perception stemmed not from any actual life changes, but from my ability to convincingly appear to project a particular persona. Through these experiments, I came to realize the extent to which you can make the system work for or against you through the mindful manipulation of your personal aesthetic. A strategic appearance allows you to seize social capital, regardless of other potentially conflicting realities.

Often times, it isn't until we deliberately play dress-up that we realize the power of fashion. I did not anticipate the extent to which I would become simultaneously invisible and conspicuous to different audiences with each distinct look. I was surprised how radically my perceptions of my own attractiveness shifted with each experiment—sometimes positively in ways I hadn't anticipated. Or how not only my state of mind but also my movement and behavior changed.

The anonymity of the street rarely asks for credentials beyond appearance. How we look provides contextual clues that help us read one another and communicate more effectively. Your image can even become your primary currency (just ask any Instagram star), and the choices you make in self-fashioning can drastically enhance or limit your social mobility. Stepping outside of yourself gives you permission to behave out of character, which ushers in previously inaccessible encounters and realizations. Reality, belief, and illusion intersect as we parade across the stage of the modern metropolitan street. The items with which we choose to associate are a visual statement of belonging and distinction, status and aspiration. Material objects allow us to customize our identities and personalize our brands.

Whether cloaked in a veil, sporting a fanny pack, or hobbling along in rhinestone stilettos, our appearance is mediated by visual signs and social indicators, all of which operate in an image-centric society that shamelessly rewards and penalizes on sight—whether we want to accept and admit it or not (many remain in denial about the larger influence of image). Regardless of our affinity or disdain for fashion, the way we dress largely determines our group belonging. We are all characters in the larger social drama, and the way in which we fashion our bodies and play our individual roles not only invests or strips power from each individual but also reappropriates that power in the larger social order.

As I found in my experiments, the significance of style is not relegated to the realm of the privileged. Reducing image to either a dangerous trap or a marker of excess limits its transformative capabilities. Fear not: thinking about how you look is not an exercise in mindless consumerism. It doesn't automatically reprogram your TiVo to record *What Not to Wear* or make you skip straight to the Sunday Styles section of *The New York Times*. Rather, approaching your appearance with the experimental agility of a startup allows you to (re)fashion the possibilities of your life. The physical trying on of selves is a creative act that has the power to rebuke realities we previously saw as a permanent consequence of birth. Our identities are designed, not inherited.

A powerful appearance is not automatically granted with a pair of heels or guaranteed with every facelift. It does not always wear a suit and it has been known to leave the house without makeup. And pleasure is derived as much from the potential we imagine as it is the current face staring back at us. The power of image is situated in the possibilities and alternate realities—plucked from storybooks and street blogs alike—that are repositioned within the visible context of our lives. In many ways, playful impersonation, not some antiquated notion of authenticity, is the key to success and happiness. Your image is a renewable resource, and while each costume change may not start a revolution, it will transform your reality.

SCRUM MASTER CHEAT SHEET

It is possible to hack your image for maximum happiness without becoming a fashionista. Here's how.

☞ **REDEFINE AUTHENTICITY.** If this chapter did anything, I hope it gave you permission to stop obsessing over whether you're authentic enough. Because you are. It's a complex word and one that our closets don't easily simplify. We all aspire to be our true selves, and yet the elusive, individualistic nature of authenticity makes a true self impossible to uniformly define or permanently embody. Knowing the self is a dynamic process, and dressing in a way that feels authentic is often complicated by context-specific demands. The way we're expected to appear does not always reflect the self with which we most identify, and yet we must find a way to reconcile that feeling of "this is me" with these social and professional pressures.

So rest assured: Choosing to embrace a visual identity that is not traditionally associated with the biographical realities into which you were born does not call your authenticity into question. You may be buttoned up with clients and more bohemian with friends, but one isn't more "real" than the other. Embracing fashion as a tool for self-discovery and personal expression helps you radiate a different type of authenticity—one that recognizes you are a multidimensional creature in a constant state of flux. You *are* the self you project; it is real. It may seem counterintuitive, but projecting authenticity requires both experimentation and reinvention.

☞ **PLAY DRESS-UP.** I often asked my students to temporarily step out of their own "skin," not unlike the costumed experiments I performed. They were tasked with going into a public place of their choosing with a self-assigned objective—making a purchase from an upscale store, applying for a job, asking for directions—while deliberately altering a particular aspect of their appearance. They were allowed to commit to the exercise at their own level of comfort, with some changing one small aspect (like applying or removing makeup), while others completely adopted an entirely different subculture. Regardless of how radical or banal the changes seemed to others, the exercise was often a very dramatic experience for the student. Shifting their public presentation of self—even slightly—altered their sense of confidence and relationship with the outside world. As a result, they often recognized many elements of their identities that they previously took for granted (like an attachment to the display of long hair as a demonstration of femininity, or the realization of how dependent they are on one particular beauty product for social comfort). The process is as therapeutic as it is enlightening, as witnessed by my own series of dress-up experiments. Our hang-ups, dependencies, and desires are more wrapped up in our appearance than we often acknowledge.

Challenge yourself to play around with the visual variables that define you and that you normally take for granted. Slightly change up your usual work image on a day you're presenting or interfacing with a higher-up and see how the exchange unfolds, observing any changes (you may want to repeat a few times to control for any additional variables). Or, if you're feeling more daring, choose a persona that's completely foreign to you and venture out. Chances are you'll feel nervous and uncomfortable at first, but the anonymity and separation from your usual identity may liberate and surprise you.

☞ **ADOPT A UNIFORM.** What if I told you that getting rid of half your wardrobe would reduce your likelihood of "nothing to wear" syndrome and diminish stress around getting dressed? That's the theory behind a capsule wardrobe—otherwise known as a small collection of versatile basics. Curating a highly specific yet extremely flexible wardrobe reduces the number of items you sift through each day and also gives you more options (because everything coordinates). It allows you to do more with less. A capsule wardrobe is just one of the ways to create a uniform for yourself. Developing a uniform isn't about looking the same every single day. It's a sleek, low-maintenance approach to creating subtle style variations by mixing and matching a tight, precisely chosen selection of pieces. And it's also a direct path to minimalism and streamlining your life. (Note that a uniform is not at odds with playing dress-up. Even as you experiment, you want a solid aesthetic foundation to anchor you.) Refine whatever aspect of your appearance causes you trouble (or wastes your time), and develop regular go-to looks. Regardless of what type of uniform you create, I recommend two key ingredients: (1) expert tailoring, which can make even a cheap article of clothing look expensive, and (2) quality pieces made of elegant fabrics, which will radically transform the drape and flow of any garment—as well as how it's perceived.

If looking good doesn't motivate you, another key selling point of the uniform is the elimination of choice, which allows you to save your mental power for other, more important thoughts and actions. Having to make new choices wears down mental energy and causes decision fatigue, and a tired brain can even lead to a loss of self-control. You need to conserve and routinize whenever possible. Finding daily ways to foster repetition, like dressing in a replicable fashion, can radically improve your efficacy in other areas of life (not to mention the time you'll save). Plus, a recognizable visual brand is important in conveying a coherent, memorable message that connects with your audience. Meaning uniforms can be liberating, economical, and even socially conscious (less waste!)—and they can establish a strong sense of identity, making them far more powerful than they are boring.

THE LAZY LOWDOWN: TOP TEN CHAPTER TAKEAWAYS

1. Masks aren't just for Halloween.
2. Your possible self is the real self you have yet to actualize.
3. Playing dress-up animates possibilities and shifts self-perception.
4. Audience buy-in begins with appearance.
5. We are responsible for our own looks.
6. Chameleons are still authentic.
7. Transforming your appearance is liberating, not fickle.
8. Identity is fluid.
9. Creativity beats biography.
10. Be seen—so you can be heard.

7.

Go Virtual

LIFE, MEDIATED

*We can afford to lose money—even a lot of money. But we can't
afford to lose reputation—even a shred of reputation.*

—WARREN BUFFETT, Memo to Berkshire
Hathaway managers

Josh was ahead of his time. In 1993, when dial-up was your primary path to the Internet—if you even had a connection—he became the first person to launch an online television show, which
he aired on the video webcasting site Pseudo.com. Like many other
early Internet moguls, his company, Jupiter Communications, went
public and he made a fortune. But Josh didn't just create cutting-
edge companies: he also experimented on his own life. He threw
crazy parties that would make Warhol proud and became a fixture in the New York art and nightlife scenes. He even occasionally went out dressed as a clown with scary face paint—it was his

alter ego, "Luvvy," a name inspired by Eunice "Lovey" Howell, the wife of Thurston Howell III of *Gilligan's Island* (with which he was obsessed).[1]

Then, in 1999, in the month leading up to the turn of the Millennium, he staged one of the greatest social experiments ever, called "Quiet." He created an underground Big Brother–style bunker—complete with a gun range and an 80-foot dining table—in which he housed 100 volunteers, all of whom had to face interrogation and reveal intimate details of their lives to gain acceptance. He installed surveillance cameras around the space, and each participant had their own sleeping pod and television on which to watch the others sleeping, showering, having sex—everything was captured and broadcast. It was a voluntary digital panopticon. Everything was free, but Josh reserved the right to use participants' images however he pleased.[2] As crazy as it sounded at the time, it was essentially a precursor to several of today's extremely popular reality shows.

Josh also subjected himself to the same public scrutiny: After the Quiet project was shut down by the police and the fire department on New Year's Day, 2000, Josh launched weliveinpublic .com, which broadcast the intimacies of his day-to-day life with his live-in girlfriend, Tanya. Though they had already been together for years, the relationship could not withstand the 100-day, self-imposed fishbowl, and they broke up.

Josh's fortune went south when the dot-com bubble burst. After Tanya left him, he claimed that "Pseudo was a fake company"[3] and referred to Tanya as his "fake girlfriend"[4]—dismissing it all as part of a long-form art piece. He escaped to an apple orchard in upstate New York, which he sold in 2006, and moved to Ethiopia—where, according to him, he smoked a lot of pot.[5] Ondi Timoner, the maker of *We Live In Public*, a 2009 documentary about Josh, caught up with him in 2014. She found him broke, living in an efficiency apartment in Las Vegas, and working on his latest project, Net Band Command: a real-world version of *The Truman Show*—what he claims to have been building up to all along.[6]

An Internet pioneer you've likely never heard of, Josh Harris may seem a bit out there, toeing the line between groundbreaking innovator and performance-art spectacle. But as wacky as his experiments are, they often appeal to us in ways we haven't previously considered; they are as disturbing as they are irresistible. In 2009, Josh told *The Guardian* that we now want more than the 15 minutes of fame Warhol predicted: we want a life of everyday fame, with perma-publicity.[7] But at what cost? We sacrifice our privacy in exchange for the satisfaction we get from being looked at and the pleasure we derive from sharing personal details publicly. We are exposure obsessed, and we also crave the intimate detail of others—without necessarily wanting to know them IRL (as the kids say).

Marshall McLuhan famously argued that the medium is the message. He defined a medium as an extension of who we are— something that gives our body and person reach beyond what would otherwise be humanly possible.[8] Media don't just transmit messages, they also color them. Words uttered in a Facebook post or as an Instagram caption are understood differently than those words spoken to one individual via the telephone or in person. Same words, different effect.

You don't need to participate in one of Josh's experiments to understand that our lives are increasingly mediated by technology. Technological advancements increase the power to preserve what we say or how we look at any moment, erasing the front- and back-stage division we explored in the previous chapter—as well as any distinction between one's "real" and fabricated selves. Technology blurs audiences and spheres, making "reality" something far more rooted in imagination than physicality.

In late 2015, Julie Cordray and Nicole McCullough launched Peeple, a platform on which people leave "reviews," complete with a five-star rating system, for individuals they know, be it socially, professionally, or romantically. The founders describe the app— appropriately dubbed "Yelp for humans"[9]—as an outlet for you to shine, *or* a way of checking up on the character of your friends and neighbors. Two years earlier, in 2013, Alexandra Chong launched Lulu, another app that rates humans—only this one allows female users to rate men on their romantic and sexual performance. Critics argue that subjectivity abounds, and besides, assigning a person a numeric value is, well, wrong. Peeple seems like the ultimate confirmation of the idea that our online depiction and characterization define us—or, at the very least, inform others' perceptions of us. That representation becomes our reality, especially when we don't control it anymore.

Both apps received heavy scrutiny and pushback. As a result, by 2014, Lulu switched to an "opt-in" model, which means only men who want feedback are searchable,[10] and before it even launched in 2015, Cordray announced that Peeple would only allow positive feedback, and nothing would be posted without permission.[11]

In a technological age, we all operate within the image industry—and our image trades at a high personal price in the social exchange marketplace. This image-centric feeding frenzy fuels confusion over our "reel" versus "real" lives. We now compete with our own mediated images—our social media profiles, our online dating profiles, our virtual world avatars—and living up to our digital selves is no easy feat. In other words, your 3D self now competes with your 2D self, and your 3D self is probably not winning.

The curation and maintenance process for online identities is constant. We might untag ourselves in photos or Photoshop unflattering ones; we might promote or comment on an article that takes a vocal or controversial stance on an issue, a sort of digital activism; or we may endorse or "like" the posts of others, with the hope that we will curry the same favor in return. Or, as Bret Easton Ellis suggests when writing about "the cult of likability," blandness, conformity, and defensive behavior may dominate this new "reputation economy": "What is being erased in the reputation economy are the contradictions inherent in all of us. Those of us who reveal flaws and inconsistencies become terrifying to others, the ones to avoid."[12] Some individuals go so far as to create two separate profiles on any given social platform: one for their professional network and another for their personal lives; others separate their various personalities and identities across specific platforms—an attempt to isolate, control, and water down "reality." But despite our best efforts, we're still one person, with many facets. All of which are "real," depending on how we define it.

In the 2009 movie *Surrogates*, humans spend all their time at home and send out individual robot surrogates into the world. These relative doppelgangers are just like us—only better. They are hotter, smarter, and immune to illness and accidents. We operate them remotely, so we get to feel everything they do, but without the danger. In the future *Surrogates* imagines, it's perceived as risky—reckless, even—to operate with your "real" body rather than your surrogate. It may seem like science fiction, but the fact is, we largely already operate in this mode.

Remember when photographs were personal? And only a small group of people ever saw them? They remained hidden in an album, only to be paraded out on the rare occasions when close friends were gathered. Maybe they induced a few laughs at your expense, but chances are you never lost your job as a result. Remember when letters were written and sent directly to one person, with that handwritten artifact the only copy, likely seen by only a single pair of eyes? Remember when wherever you were physically was the only place anyone could see or interact with you?

The "looking-glass self" is a psychological concept that suggests we develop our sense of self based on the perceptions of others, and that the degree of personal insecurity you display in social situations is determined by what you believe other people think of you.[13] We reach and can be seen by thousands of people simultaneously online, making our profiles and avatars influential representations of our online identities. Narcissism—but also self-consciousness—abounds.

The thought that our image is worthy of publication and comment is at once flattering and nerve-wracking. We are struck with the harsh reality that with the glamour comes new opportunities for scrutiny. Comments and criticisms are not fact-checked by an Internet jury, or retracted when unfair, or vetted for cruelty. Accountability dissipates and anxiety mounts.

And yet, these virtual worlds can be liberating. They offer a timeout from our physical lives and create an open environment for a radical reimagining of who we are—what we look like, how we communicate, what sorts of groups we join or partnerships we form, our beliefs and desires. They offer us a chance at a second existence, or a multiplicity of selves, that can be therapeutic.

Launched in 2003, *Second Life* is a user-created virtual world. Unlike gaming platforms like *World of Warcraft*, the mass appeal of *Second Life* is not rooted in any type of formal competition. Rather, it's a creative space for designing whatever life you desire.

Your only limitations are time, imagination, and some small capital—it's free to use, but you can trade Linden Dollars, the game's currency, for various goods and services. Some users attempt to create a character in their own likeness, while others opt for something completely fantastical (on the few occasions that I've gone "inworld," as they say, I've self-presented as a unicorn). Everyone roaming about in *Second Life* is "real" in the sense that they're operated by a human and not generated by the platform. Some users describe the avatars they create as a persona to which they've long felt an attachment but for which they did not previously have an outlet, while others, like me, choose more random physicalities. Regardless, the avatar—and its actions and conversations—becomes an exploration of the user's subconscious. Of their fears, secrets, and under-explored affinities.

I often asked my students to experiment with social dynamics and the online representation of self—including gender, sexuality, and race. They could choose from personal social media profiles, a *Second Life* avatar, or another social digital platform as part of the foundation of their final project. The *Second Life* projects always offered the most dynamic and provocative results. Moving beyond the hyper-sexualization and fetish-oriented aspects the site is widely known for, many of the students explored issues that were central to their own lives. One student who was a mother explored childbirth and family: What does it mean to give birth and have a family in *Second Life*? And what does that say about our motivations and expectations in real life? Another student with physical disabilities focused her attention there: If one is in a wheelchair or physically restricted in real life, why might they choose to remain in that state in *Second Life*? And in a virtual world where everything is created, are there ethical considerations around which users have a "right" to self-present in that way? Others chose topics that touched family members or friends, like grief or depression: Anonymity allowed them to seek support and speak openly about issues they struggled with in real life. Designated confessional spaces serve as therapeutic outlets for users, regardless of the virtual nature of their avatar. Virtual gyms even exist where avatars can work out, a sort of digital conditioning for the mind-set and lifestyle users are looking to embody in their physical lives.

The students were almost always initially skeptical of these virtual worlds, perceiving them as a hobby for individuals who operate on the social fringes. But through mindful exploration, they not only learned the social norms and habits of these virtual places, but also the complex nature of their own beliefs and assumptions. These virtual spaces are just another foreign land in which one can invalidate assumptions and question who they are. After all, we learn the most about ourselves when nudged out of our comfort zones, left to navigate the unfamiliar wilds without a script.

But while virtual spaces can offer a useful outlet for self-exploration, they are not without real consequences.

In 2011, Ross Ulbricht launched a black market site called Silk Road, with the intent of allowing anyone to buy almost anything anonymously, without leaving a trace. And thanks to technology like the cryptocurrency Bitcoin and the Tor browser, which allows users to mask their location and activity and avoid a digital trail (something popularly referred to the "darknet"), Ulbricht and his users were able to operate privately—though in public—for two years. Over 70 percent of the products sold on the site were drugs, and Silk Road quickly became a billion-dollar business.[14] But it wasn't a simple black market. Several customers died from substances purchased from the site, and when Ulbricht was arrested in 2013, the trial that unfolded revealed a mysterious mess of dirty agents, conspiracy to kill, and a confusing electronic trail of concealed and mistaken identity, all of which led to his conviction in 2015.[15] Ulbricht was sentenced to life in prison with no chance of parole on seven counts, including money laundering, narcotics trafficking, continuing criminal enterprise, conspiracy to traffic in fraudulent identity documents, and computer hacking.

While at the helm of Silk Road, Ulbricht used a pseudonym: Dread Pirate Roberts (or DPR, as he was popularly called). And when Silk Road was shut down in October 2013 and Silk Road 2.0 launched the following month, its new alleged leader, Blake Benthall, also adopted the Dread Pirate Roberts pseudonym[16]— different person, same persona (Benthall was arrested in November 2014, and as of this writing, his case is still pending). The larger-than-life, made-for-Hollywood storyline is a sort of mashup of *Scarface* meets the television show *Silicon Valley*, with a dash of *The Princess Bride* (where the character of DPR originated)—a strange yet compelling combination, to say the least. The DPR Silk Road conspiracy—with its deaths, convictions, and economic heft—demonstrates how real the digital realm can be. And given the absence of the body and the ease with which technology-fueled secrecy may flourish, the biographical "reality" of the individuals involved matters far less than their virtual behavior.

Ulbricht's defense attorney, Joshua Dratel, addressed the subjective nature of reality on the Internet during his closing arguments in the trial: "The Internet denies us the opportunity to decide what is masquerade, what is truth, what is hidden."[17] But online fantasy is not without consequence, even if you aren't leading a drug-trafficking operation on the darknet. Researchers have found that the way we perceive ourselves affects our behavior. And our online behavior can play a big role in shaping our real-world actions. Whether you slip into an avatar in a virtual world like *Second Life* or an online game like *World of Warcraft*, or if you operate primarily via your digitized self across social media platforms, those interactions are more than just virtual banter. Research indicates that a mere 90 seconds spent looking at one's online avatar alters behavior patterns. For instance, if the avatar is good-looking, the user interacts in a more confident, extroverted manner. Another study found that one's online avatar also affects offline behavior. After spending time online as their avatar, the subjects were asked to choose potential dates from a series of photographs. Those with attractive avatars chose better-looking mates than those with less-attractive avatars, regardless of the appearance of the participant.[18] Similar studies indicate much the same results: users with tall avatars and users that exercise in the platform behave with self-assurance similar to that of actual tall and fit people. Those with shorter or lazier avatars showed no corresponding real-world increase in self-assurance.[19]

An attractive, lively online persona feeds directly into our self-perception and confidence level when we are face-to-face with actual humans. This means that the life you create for yourself online matters, but for reasons beyond the usual warnings (we've all been cautioned that employers look at your social media and that the Internet leaves a forever footprint). What is often ignored, though far more important in the long run, is how your digital self-creation and expression influences your belief (or lack thereof) in your real-world self. In short, if your online persona is hot, healthy, and confident, your real world self will also likely experience an ego boost—whether it's warranted or not. Those are some pretty powerful pixels.

SCRUM MASTER CHEAT SHEET

Love 'em or hate 'em, our online identities are not disappearing anytime soon. And you don't need to own a company to understand the importance of a virtual presence—just as every company is now a tech company, every person needs a technological counterpart. Whatever your platform(s) of choice, here are a few basic principles that will help you to thrive amid the digital chaos.

☞ **REAP THE DIGITAL ROI.** At this point, virtual identities probably sound like a lot of work—an unnecessary headache or a landmine waiting to trap and embarrass you. But digital platforms can actually work to your advantage. Whether you strive to be an influencer or just want to stay informed, online participation is valuable for far more than rampant selfie flashing.

One study found that the one thing that distinguishes the happiest 10 percent of people is the strength of their social relationships.[20] And while there's plenty of legitimate criticism about how technology can erode social bonds, it does allow us to connect with more people, more frequently, significantly raising the ceiling for our connection-related happiness quotient. How? It's estimated that the average American has from two to six close social contacts,[21] and it is through our close, intimate connections that information, influence, and innovation are thought to be diffused. Dunbar's number, generally estimated to be around 150, is the theoretical number of people with whom we can maintain stable relationships.[22] But our larger, weaker ties are equally important, as they connect us to people we don't know well, which offers a larger pool for networking and influence.

Your online presence allows you to maintain and build a network that stretches far beyond your physical limitations. This network can also prove useful in bypassing hierarchical gatekeepers and accessing otherwise out-of-reach people, be it a celebrity, a thought leader, or just a customer service representative. Many will respond to online social pings faster than calls, texts, or emails. In 1994, marketing guru Seth Godin wrote the book *Email Addresses of the Rich & Famous,* which offered the personal email addresses of everyone from Ross Perot to Billy Idol to the voice of Barney.[23] While that book now seems quaint, it was revolutionary when it launched. Fortunately, you no longer need to buy a directory to reap the digital networking rewards.

☞ **CURB REPUTATION-DAMAGING RECKLESSNESS.** Publicity. Most of us want it to varying degrees. But the old adage that there's no such thing as bad publicity doesn't quite hold up. Digital slip-ups abound. We will never forget the Anthony Weiner sexting scandal, which became known as "Weinergate" (followed by Weiner's even more astonishing "Carlos Danger" incident). There's also the "Cisco Fatty" story: Cisco offered 22-year-old Connor Riley a job, and while pondering the offer, she tweeted that while she'd get a "fatty paycheck," she would hate the work. Unsurprisingly, the offer was revoked.[24]

So how should you behave in a world without walls, where there is no clear distinction between public and private? What does it mean to be a stranger? A friend? What's real and what's fake? Virtual interactions are often perceived as intimate in ways that mimic our physical relationships. And the rules of engagement are anything but clear in a space paved with shades of grey.

Life on the screen is complicated. And the decisions you make with regard to your digital life matter, so why leave that to chance? In an effort to avoid virtual foot-in-mouth syndrome, it pays to have an online agenda. Forethought and conscious decision making trumps careless digital bleed-outs. What do we hope to gain from our virtual interactions? Is it worth whatever attention or exposure we receive? While I hope you never find yourself in a situation as mortifying or damning as Weiner or Riley did, chances are you will—sooner or later—do something less than graceful on the virtual stage. So you are faced with a digital dilemma: sterilize or personalize?

Remind yourself that just because you can share everything, all the time, it doesn't mean it's a good idea. Ask yourself if you would want to create a public mural of whatever you're putting out into cyberspace—because online actions that might seem innocuous can get blown up quickly and seriously. Digital gaffes linger and sting far more than a misspoken word to a colleague.

In an effort to avoid going down in a ball of viral flames, it's easy to overcompensate and strip yourself of your distinguishing elements. So do you become a bland, innocuous avatar of yourself, or do you put yourself out there and choose to stand for something? Bret Easton Ellis reminds us that the "negative and the difficult" are also sometimes "attached to the genuinely interesting, the compelling, the unusual."[25] So give yourself permission to be a real, whole person. You are not a one-dimensional being. Keep it human.

☛ **PIMP YOUR PROFILE.** We primp and manicure our bodies on repeat, and daily maintenance is required of even the most visually modest among us. But image management has become exponentially more complex as we self-present online. You've picked out your outfit for the day, but what about your virtual profiles? Does that photo make your ego look big? Did someone tag you overnight in an image that reveals TMI? As sociologist Zygmunt Bauman put it, "Identity is a sentence to lifelong hard labor."[26] And your virtual identity is no exception. The pressure we feel to visually perform in our physical, embodied lives is multiplied as we—and everyone we know—has access to our image 24/7. Some feel so much pressure to look perfect in their online photos that they transform their physical bodies through invasive procedures (a.k.a., the "Facebook facelift"[27]).

We're constantly told that our online personas are our brand. And yet, we have many facets to our identities. The way we interact with our families, our work personas, and the various subcultures and niche groups we're a part of all necessitate and nurture different aspects of our personalities. Each dimension is "us," however disparate they may seem. So, when it comes time to represent yourself virtually, you may question which *you* to embody. Some people use their online personas as an outlet for expressing their alter ego, and while that works in spaces like *Second Life*, more mainstream virtual sites demand some restraint when it comes to living out fantasies. Tweeting about medical issues while self-presenting as a pin-up doll can send mixed messages and weaken your voice not only in the virtual world but also in person. And yet, no one wants to look like a cheesy stock photograph, so create an aesthetic where you feel alive: not Glamour Shot you, but everyday you—only slightly better.

THE LAZY LOWDOWN: TOP TEN CHAPTER TAKEAWAYS

1. We live in public, even in private.
2. Technology anchors reality in imagination, not physicality.
3. The medium is the message. Listen up.
4. Maintain your surrogates—or someone else will.
5. Don't set yourself up for 3D failure: keep your 2D self in check.

6. There's value in your virtual network. Maximize the returns.
7. Bold is better than bland. Be a whole person (but one you can be proud of).
8. Go on a cyberspace odyssey: get lost in a foreign frontier of self-exploration and discovery.
9. Digital deeds have real-world repercussions.
10. Don't be a Weiner. Mediate with caution.

8.

Hustle and Grow

Happiness is not in the mere possession of money; it lies in the joy of achievement, in the thrill of creative effort.

—FRANKLIN ROOSEVELT, inaugural speech,
March 4, 1933

Larry wasn't born with a silver spoon in his mouth. In fact, his life was anything but privileged. Born in 1944 New York to a single mother, he was adopted by his aunt and uncle as a baby and raised in Chicago. After his aunt died, Larry dropped out of college and moved to California.

Larry started hacking and playing around with software development while he was still a teenager, eventually writing his own programs. Computers appealed to him because they were rational, logical—and working for himself was fun *and* lucrative.[1] Larry worked as a freelance programmer and refined his skills for the next decade. He read an IBM paper about a new, more efficient type of database for storing information and, in 1977, linked up with co-founders Bob Miner and Ed Oates to build a prototype of what's called a relational database. The CIA signed on as his first client.[2] Clearly, Larry was onto something.

From a man whose life could have taken a far less impressive path, the Oracle Corporation was born. Oracle went on to create the software and hardware that powers many of the companies we rely on today. As of 2015, Forbes lists Larry Ellison as the fifth-richest person in the world, and Oracle as the seventeenth most valuable brand. His $50 billion net worth affords him noteworthy lifestyle excesses, like his $200 million home, $200 million yacht, and his own personal $300 million Hawaiian island.[3]

There are few contemporary rags-to-riches stories quite like Larry Ellison's. Despite a challenging upbringing and little advanced formal academic training, he's now one of the richest guys in the world. He achieved this status not because of where he was born or who his family is, but because of his ability to test himself and push his own limits. Yes, pedigree and silver spoons can and do open many doors. But so does hustle.

In fact, pulling yourself up by the bootstraps is a great American tradition. In 1835, a man named Andrew was born into poverty in Scotland and later emigrated to the United States with his parents. At the tender age of 13, he entered the workforce, raking in a whopping $1.20 a week for over 70 hours of work at a cotton mill. A few years later, he worked as a telegraph messenger, more than doubling his pay to $2.50 per week. By age 18, he was up to $4 per week as he launched his career at the Pennsylvania Railroad Company—a booming industry at the time.[4]

Andrew was curious, loved to read, and was a shrewd networker, cultivating meaningful relationships with his seniors[5]— qualities that further set him on the path to success. He invested what money he had early and often and ultimately made his fortune in the steel industry, eventually selling his company to J. P. Morgan.

Andrew not only didn't come from privilege, but he was quick to criticize those who inherited their wealth, including the British monarchy.[6] He was also an outspoken critic in his disdain for the accumulation of wealth without a proportional commitment to philanthropic pursuits and the larger enrichment of society. In his 1889 essay, "Wealth," Andrew writes that "the man who dies leaving behind many millions of available wealth, which was his to administer during life, will pass away 'unwept, unhonored, and unsung' . . . 'The man who dies thus rich dies disgraced.'"[7]

Some consider Andrew Carnegie the greatest philanthropist ever. The man who once worked for pennies a day eventually amassed enough wealth to give over $350 million to charity before he died—more than 90 percent of his net worth.[8] (Carnegie would, no doubt, approve of Mark Zuckerberg's 2015 commitment to eventually give away 99 percent of his Facebook shares, worth around $45 billion, through his charitable fund, the Chan Zuckerberg Initiative.[9] And despite the perception that Ellison is all luxury jets and private islands, he is one of 40 individuals to sign the Giving Pledge, which promises to give 95 percent of his wealth to charity.) Carnegie saw money as a means to enrich life for the greater populace—not personal gain. Wealth alone was not his end game. He wrote:

> Man does not live by bread alone. I have known millionaires
> starving for lack of the nutriment which alone can sustain all that
> is human in man, and I know workmen, and many so-called poor
> men, who revel in luxuries beyond the power of those million-
> aires to reach. It is the mind that makes the body rich. There is
> no class so pitiably wretched as that which possesses money and

nothing else. Money can only be the useful drudge of things im-measurably higher than itself. My aspirations take a higher flight . . . the joys of the mind . . . the things of the spirit.[10]

And yet, money *is* important. So let's address the controver-sial question: Whether you give it away or use it for indulgences, does money make you happy? Perhaps you've heard the oft-cited research finding that winning the lottery doesn't produce lasting happiness.[11] When it comes to money and happiness, it's less about specific numbers and more about the choices that surround those numbers. Studies find that the amount of money you make matters less than how you spend it, and while money alone can't buy hap-piness, strategic spending can significantly enhance your well-being.[12] According to the 2010 Second European Quality of Life Survey, the state of deprivation is more than just a lack of luxury—it is something that radically reduces your quality of life and mental and physical well-being.[13] As you might imagine, deprivation means going without basics, like heat or regular meals, but it's also defined as going without new furniture, new clothes, or even va-cation. When looking at happiness, sometimes luxuries are not so different from necessities.

And even if Carnegie's philanthropic mandates feel too ex-treme for you, remember that the phrase "giving is receiving" is far more than cliché. Altruism, even on a modest scale, gives our lives meaning and direction. In fact, studies show that spending money on others boosts happiness more than spending it on your-self.[14] But when you're just trying to get by, giving away money can seem more reckless than righteous. Fortunately, you don't need millions to reap the rewards of altruism. Small investments in other people can have the biggest rewards—just think of the money (and hassle) you'd save the person parked next to you if you added some change to their expired meter.

As Ellison and Carnegie know well, few startups are given millions of dollars from day one. Instead, they're forced to bootstrap and make the best of whatever resources currently exist to prove their mettle to investors. Ellison and Carnegie didn't lean on family inheritance or investor capital when they started. They had to become financial MacGyvers and improvise their way to success.

Working on a small budget isn't all negative: not all money is created equal, and there is such a thing as "bad money." For startups, things like unfavorable terms or dilution of equity can quickly turn a dream investment into a nightmare. When you're just trying to keep the company alive, it can seem like all money is good, but accepting short-term investment at the cost of long-term control can ruin your prospects before you even start.

We've all encountered the equivalent of "bad money" in our own lives, like loans from friends or family with unrealistic expectations attached. The key lesson to take from these experiences is to avoid myopia at all costs—even when desperate. I've been down on my luck enough times to know that when you're struggling to make rent or buy food for the week, you'll take help from wherever it comes and deal with the consequences later. It's called survival. But no matter what, look at money as part of a long-game trajectory, even if it means making sacrifices in the short term.

And I'm not just referring to 401ks and savings accounts—we've all been lectured on the merits of saving for the future. I'm talking about rethinking where, when, and how you take in money today, and how that can negatively affect not only your financial standing but also your well-being, far into the future. Taking the high-paying job you'll hate instead of going back to school to pursue your dream might seem like the responsible thing to do, but is it sustainable? How long can you endure something that makes you miserable—and at what cost? Everything suffers when what we do doesn't make us excited to wake up in the morning. So whether that means changing jobs or restructuring priorities to make more time for a passion project or hobby, do it—you'll thank yourself later.

Accepting outside capital isn't the only path to success. Some startups forgo venture money altogether or bootstrap for a prolonged period of time. The now-famous dating site PlentyofFish was a one-man operation run out of an apartment for years before the founder finally hired a team, eventually gaining hundreds of millions in revenue, all without ever accepting venture money. They eventually sold to Match Group for over half a billion dollars.[15] Clothing retailer Nasty Gal started as a vintage eBay shop and functioned independently for over five years, growing its profitability to tens of millions of dollars before taking any outside capital.[16] Tough Mudder was launched with $10,000 of the founders' personal savings and has been profitable every year since its launch in 2009, now bringing in over $100 million per year—all without outside investment.[17]

Of course bootstrapping means different things to different people. For some, it's about a "friends and family" round—which means asking people in your network for an investment in exchange for equity (knowing there's a good chance they'll never get that money back). It's not dissimilar from the "loans" we might take from our families when we're still getting it together—both sides know that parents are probably not going to see that money again. For others, it means relying on money saved up from a high-paying job. Some entrepreneurs start in finance or some other lucrative field, create a nest egg, then eventually go out on their own (though they will tell you it's often hard to adjust to the lifestyle change). Still (lucky) others have a trust fund to fuel their venture.

I am no stranger to bootstrapping. Like Carnegie and Ellison, my journey didn't begin anywhere glamorous. I was born in Waterloo, Iowa, an industrial Midwestern town. My mother raised me alone, and, due to political complications (and other drama worthy of a book unto itself), I've never met my Iranian father. Any single-parent family will tell you it's hard. My mom's father was a truck driver and her mother worked at a retail store, so there was no family money to fall back on. What there was, however, was government assistance, which helped us meet basic needs while I was young. When I was still a baby, we moved into the Hillside Apartments: a 32-unit apartment complex on Waterloo's rough East Side, where my neighbors were as colorful as you'd expect for a place that cost less than $100 per month. I attended Head Start. We rode the public bus until I was seven and did without other luxuries like color TV and various household conveniences until I was much older.

The rest of my story may sound like some sort of right-wing advertisement: I studied hard, joined every board/club/activity I could, developed creative talents, found ways to give back to the community from a young age (thanks to my mother's persistence), and never forgot the gritty place from which I started.

I went on to enroll in years of expensive private schooling—thanks in large part to scholarships and loans—where I was surrounded by extreme wealth. And yet, looking back, I was largely oblivious to the financial disparity between me and my peers. Whenever people met me, they assumed I was financially privileged. Then, after learning I was not, they resorted to, "Well, you're lucky." (And you know how unsavory I find that term.) But their words only made me work harder. Refusing to settle for the circumstances of my birth, I instead opted to hustle.

And here's the good news: As contrived as it may sound, overcoming these challenges is the greatest gift I've ever received. No matter where you begin—whether in privilege or poverty—and regardless of the obstacles you encounter along the way, it's the strategy you hone and deploy, not the quantifiable wealth into which you're born, that determines your sustainable happiness level.

Bootstrapping may seem like an unappealing option. But many entrepreneurs who've operated without venture capital argue in favor of the self-sufficiency nurtured by going it alone, without a financial safety net and with no large infusions of cash. Bootstrapping breeds a survival mentality. It makes you tougher, savvier, and teaches you hard lessons fast, whether you're ready or not.

But you don't need to be launching a company to understand and benefit from the bootstrapping mentality. Getting creative with how you spend your money and where you source it is a crucial way of improving your life—without a trust fund or a six-figure job. And it's something every person, regardless of their current financial position, can embrace. So how do you get started?

Let me first ask you this: Can a startup reach space? Elon Musk, founder of SpaceX, Tesla, and PayPal says, why not? Musk launched SpaceX in 2002 with the goal of creating reusable rockets at a fraction of the usual cost, with a bold long-term vision of colonizing space, with Mars as the first target planet. Ultimately, this new approach to rocket manufacturing aims to make space more accessible to more people. To achieve the reusable rocket goals, Musk and his team looked at the old model for aerospace manufacturing and decided they could do it better. SpaceX reasoned that the old model of too many contractors necessitated high profit margins and thereby slowed the process and squashed innovation—while also costing much, much more. He brought much of the manufacturing in house.[18] This resulted in less bureaucracy, more internal "doing" and creating, greater output, and wider accessibility. SpaceX took a traditional, bureaucratic industry—aerospace—and approached it like any scrappy startup would. They inverted assumptions and challenged a "business as usual" approach.

Musk wasn't focused on cutting corners and tightening belts when he began SpaceX, though. Rather, he examined and re-imagined the widely accepted process, then got creative with how to do each step better—and subsequently cheaper. From engines to launch operations, no segment of the process was too miniscule or inconsequential to innovate. Similarly, SpaceX company culture allows for continual testing and cost cutting. The startup mentality of SpaceX is vastly different from the culture of NASA and government projects. Yes, Musk has money. A lot of it, thanks to PayPal. But he also has the courage—or rather the audacity—to push the limits of what's possible.

To be clear, bootstrapping isn't really about doing without—it's about being smarter about how you allocate your resources. Take outsourcing. Much has been written about the benefit of delegating tasks in your life, and yet many resist it—whether out of a desire to retain control or a mistaken assessment of value. But the bottom line is, how much is your time worth? A refusal to outsource—whether it's your laundry or your whole legal department—will eventually wear you down. Everyone's capacity is limited. How will you spend your time and energy?

Entrepreneurs tend to have a strong understanding of the value of their time. Their focus is on work that moves their business forward, not time-consuming and unpleasant non-work tasks. So non-work tasks that don't make them happy are quickly abandoned or outsourced. But it's easy to lose sight of the value of your time when you are a salaried employee. We often think that outsourcing is the province of the uber-rich or celebrities. We shame ourselves (or others) for being lazy for not doing mundane tasks. But in reality, when you outsource, you're buying yourself time—time to be more productive on work that will potentially pay off in a way that housework never will, or time to do the things you love with people you care about. When considering outsourcing, you should be looking at lifetime earnings and personal happiness, not just the tedious task at hand. It's less about debating need vs. want, and more about embracing a "time is money" mentality.

In a *60 Minutes* interview, Charlie Rose asked Bill Gates how he found the time to do everything from fathering to running companies to starting foundations to voracious reading on subjects as niche as fertilizer. Gates's response: "I don't mow the lawn."[19] Touché, Bill. In other words, choose your focus carefully—if something doesn't move you forward or make you happy, outsource it. No one ever saved the world by mowing the lawn.

That's certainly not to say that everything we do needs to have epic global consequences. But our work should satisfy a need or desire in a meaningful way, whether it's for the greater good or just our own well-being. Or better put: It should make your life either richer or easier.

My first foray into paid delegation was in grad school, while I was still completely broke. I was in the thick of writing my dissertation when I realized it would take me at least an extra semester to graduate if I didn't change the way I was working. I was teaching several classes, working a part-time consulting job, and researching and writing my dissertation. As part of my fieldwork, I conducted hours of interviews, which I audio-recorded and later transcribed. The transcription required no additional thinking or analysis but took the most time. I also had to format the document with hyper-specificity—again, not something that contributed in any meaningful way to the content. And so, out of desperation, I did something none of my peers were doing: I hired an assistant. He was an undergraduate friend of a friend, and I enlisted him to take those tasks off my hands so I could focus on completing the actual manuscript. This saved me hundreds of hours and—most importantly—allowed me to graduate that semester and not incur additional enrollment fees. The outsourcing more than paid for itself.

Around two years later, I found myself once again buried in an endless to-do list, with the mundane tasks preventing me from focusing on the projects that would push me to the next level. So one day, I made a list of all the things I wished I could delegate. I began to salivate just looking at it. Oh, what a luxury it would be to hire an assistant. But people in my financial position didn't have assistants, I told myself. Every month it was a struggle just to pay my rent. Then I did some creative problem solving. What if I *didn't* hire someone full time? What if it was just a few hours a week? And what if I offered a very modest hourly rate? Would that appeal to any truly qualified person?

Working in my favor was the fact that we were in a terrible recession. So when I went to old, reliable Craigslist to post my ad, I received over 200 responses in a matter of days, each one more impressively credentialcd than the last. I whittled the applicant pool down to 20, then 3. To help me make my final decision, I used an unconventional tactic: I asked each of the applicants to write a biographical essay. There were no length requirements, no format they had to follow. I wanted to see how they expressed themselves (I needed some basic writing and communication skills), but most importantly, I wanted to understand who they were as human beings. What defined, challenged, humbled, and motivated them. When I told friends about the exercise, some laughed and others accused me of wasting the applicants' time. But I disagreed. And more importantly, the applicants disagreed. The personal stories they offered me were both sacred and intimate. There was a reverence about how they delivered and presented them, as well as a shyness—after all, I was a relative stranger learning very personal details.

If my company had been further along or my resources more plentiful, I would've hired all three. But since that was not possible, I had to select only one. And yet, it was a bonding experience for each of us. I kept in touch with and advised one of the women for several years. And the woman I did hire (the one who walked into the first interview wearing a white ruffled shirt and immediately announced, "I don't know why I wore this. I look like a pirate.") continued to work with me for many years. In fact, we grew so close that she still remains my lost phone contact number and is a co-signer on one of my bank accounts. We even send each other happy anniversary greetings on the date we started working together.

Needless to say, this was not really a time when I was in any position to take vacations. Flights, hotel rooms, meals out—none of those things were part of my budget. Once again, I started creative problem solving. I listed my small-but-charming Manhattan apartment on a home exchange website, and suddenly I was inundated with daily offers from across the globe. People with gorgeous homes, many of whom included use of their car, wanted to come to Manhattan. It was like a free Airbnb (before anyone knew about Airbnb). All I had to do was get from point A to point B, then I could live with virtually no additional expenses. I'd gamed the vacation system.

Within a matter of months, I went from drowning in work and feeling trapped by the confines of my financial situation to sharing the workload with capable, wonderful people and gaining access to dream vacation spots, all for very minimal costs and without any influx of capital. For several more years my bank account remained unimpressive, and I continued to live without many creature comforts, but it still felt like I was winning at life.

I'd bootstrapped my way to happiness. While the right money cleverly spent can lead to happiness, success cannot be measured in dollar signs alone.

SCRUM MASTER CHEAT SHEET

Living lean doesn't mean clinging to every penny. Even when finances are tight, you still don't need to live in deprivation. Here's how to do more with less, without compromising well-being.

☞ **INVEST IN HAPPINESS.** Tech moguls get a bad rap when it comes to flaunting their riches. And in many cases, rightfully so. But not all tech founders use their money for extravagances. Some, like Vimeo founder Zach Klein, invest their energy and resources into creating communal experiences. Klein purchased 50 acres of forest for a few hundred thousand dollars in upstate New York and created a series of off-the-grid experiences for friends and eventually the larger community to share.[20] Access to some initial capital allowed him to purchase the land, but what he created with that otherwise empty space continues to evolve, thrive, and nourish not only him, but the growing community that now attaches itself to that space.

Studies prove again and again that buying experiences pays back in happiness dividends. A physical item will likely break or fade, but an experience endures, creating memories and personal bonds. For entrepreneurs, money isn't just for buying stuff; it's more of a tool that generates opportunity—or, in the case of Klein, more sustainable happiness. And when you reframe it that way, each expenditure is assessed differently, not just for its immediate value or enjoyment, but for how it fits into your bigger strategic life puzzle.

☛ **MAXIMIZE HUMAN CAPITAL.** For many years I mused that I wanted a life sponsor—someone to help bankroll all my creative pursuits. A patron of sorts. Then I realized I already had several—albeit in a slightly different format. Entrepreneurs seek funding from venture capitalists (or VCs) via formal presentations and term sheets, but everyday people can have investors, too. But rather than check writers, they are our strategic advisors and unofficial mentors. They're the individuals who invest time in sharing life lessons and doling out advice. They include us in their lives and make introductions—or they simply counsel us when we're down.

This isn't just everyday "networking." Enlisting life investors involves relationship building that goes far beyond a business card exchange, a LinkedIn request, or a casual coffee. Your relationships with these life investors evolve, and there may be times when these relationships are more intimate or distant than others. But for the relationship to really work, there must be times when what you bring to the equation enriches the investors' lives as well (investors aren't just selfless altruists, after all). Chances are you already have a few life VCs, but you may not be maximizing the return on those relationships. No, this is not a ploy to exploit or manipulate the people in your life. Quite the opposite. It is a thoughtful strategy to exchange maximum rewards with the abundance of human capital that surrounds you.

☛ **GET YOUR HUSTLE ON.** Defy Ventures is a nonprofit that invests in individuals the rest of society is not betting on: formerly and currently incarcerated men and women. Why? They recognize that with a few small tweaks, many former drug dealers and gang leaders have the qualities to be successful entrepreneurs. So they transform the hustle of this underserved population by offering them training, mentoring, and the chance to earn financial investment—and with great results: the program boasts a recidivism rate of less than 3 percent (a tremendous difference from the 75 percent national average).[21]

Hustling is often the X factor when it comes to edging out a competitor. It's the human element that money alone can't account for. The Defy entrepreneurs can't compete with the pedigrees that surround them in the marketplace, but they more than make up for it with their savvy agility, scrappy resourcefulness, and indefatigable drive. Whatever you're working toward in every corner of life, don't underestimate the power of down-and-dirty, don't-cost-nothin' hustling.

THE LAZY LOWDOWN: TOP TEN CHAPTER TAKEAWAYS

1. Believe Andrew Carnegie: it is the mind that makes the body rich.
2. Money can buy happiness. If you spend wisely.
3. The alternative to luxury isn't always deprivation. Redefine necessity.
4. Be a financial MacGyver: make something from nothing.
5. "Bad money" is a myopic trap. Avoid.
6. Bootstrapping makes you financially nimble. And flexibility pays.
7. No one saved the world by mowing the lawn. Outsource when possible.
8. Don't measure success in dollar signs.
9. Find your life VCs and create a feedback loop of value.
10. Hustle trumps pedigree. Get moving.

9.

The Partnership Puzzle

BE YOUR OWN MATCHMAKER

Don't be a lone wolf.
—Seth Bannon, "Mistakes You Should Never Make"

Burt picked up Roxanne hitchhiking in Maine in 1984. Roxanne was a single mother, while Burt was a modest beekeeper enjoying the simple life. That serendipitous, movie-worthy meet-cute sparked the beginning of an epic romantic and professional partnership. Their lives settled into a rhythm, and each person had a respective role: He minded the bees, while she transformed the beeswax into products—first candles, then lip balm and beyond. They sold their wares at craft fairs with increasing success, eventually turning their small business into the multimillion-dollar company Burt's Bees.

But alas, they did not live happily ever after. Instead, Burt Shavitz and Roxanne Quimby did what many partners do: they broke up. Roxanne bought out Burt. And when Burt's Bees sold to Clorox for $900 million, Roxanne pocketed $300 million, while Burt retained only $4 million and chose to go back to living in a converted turkey coop in Maine.[1]

Whether you're starting a company or a family, partnerships are hard. They say business partners are like spouses: you're with them every day, for better or worse, in sickness and in health. And in business and romance alike, there's usually a honeymoon phase: it's all rosy at the beginning, until reality settles in and the illusion of perfection crumbles. Across all contexts, partnerships—even the good ones—are work. The small grudges and the differences of opinion take their toll. But despite all the hurdles and headaches, partnerships can be one of the most rewarding and worthy ventures in our lives. And they are a key factor in lasting happiness.

It's no coincidence that many of the most famous companies are a result of partnerships. Sometimes one of the partners steals the show: Warren Buffett overshadows Charlie Munger, but they collaborated for over half a century. Bill Gates elbowed his way ahead of Paul Allen—and though that partnership ended acrimoniously with Gates as the clear winner, each still recognizes the unique talents of the other, the combination of which made Microsoft such a success. With Steve Jobs and Steve Wozniak, Jobs is the dominant name and legacy, but it was Wozniak's technical chops that gave Jobs something brilliant to market. Some duos are so integrated that their names are inseparable: Lewis and Clark. Wilbur and Orville. Hewlett and Packard. Watson and Crick. Ben and Jerry.

Partnerships are not just about strengths meeting strengths. A big part of the collaborative brew is the successful management of weaknesses, egos, and vulnerabilities. Each individual drags their skill sets—and their baggage—to the table. But the baggage is not necessarily something to overcome. Sometimes it can even bring out the best in each individual—it can act as a sort of complementary catalyst. Perhaps one partner's insecurities cultivate patience and attentiveness in the other, while that partner's need for space nurtures a newfound independence in the other. Because like plus like doesn't often result in relationship magic. The brilliance lies in the gentle tension. The slight difference in perspective. The ability to tease out ideas and qualities in the other person (and in ourselves) that we didn't know were there.

I've had my fair share of both business partners and boyfriends over the years, and what makes someone a good partner—in either camp—is surprisingly similar. Amazon CEO Jeff Bezos says he approached his search for a life partner in much the same way he did his business. He even went so far as to create a flowchart for his dating prospects. His top criterion? "I wanted a woman who could get me out of a Third World prison. Life's too short to hang out with people who aren't resourceful."[2] Sexiness is great, but scrappiness and practical know-how—not to mention a big helping of humor—go a long way in both love and business.

And yet, of all the aspects of our life, perhaps partnerships, romance, and love seem most at odds with the startup approach. We meet by chance, right? And we either click or not, right? And then it either works or it doesn't. Trouble is, that doesn't give you much say in the matter. In love, as in life, we're looking to "close the deal"—whether it's marriage, or just getting them to say yes to dinner. Whatever the goal, there's a market in which we operate, and it's far more than merely chance that determines the eventual outcome.

Most people crave companionship of some sort. And no wonder, as it is the single biggest indicator of long-term, sustainable health and happiness. (In fact, research suggests that *not* having close social ties is the equivalent of smoking or obesity in terms of its negative impact on health.)[3] But like entrepreneurship, romance—and partnership in general—is risky business. There's no "safe" route for the pursuit of either (no matter how many flow-charts you create). The way we learn to love and connect most fully is the same way startups succeed: they take a leap of faith, coupled with a commitment to everyday tedium. Entrepreneurship and marriage (or its equivalent) can both be intoxicating and thrill-ing, yet they're anchored in the daily grind of unsexy realities.

So what does success mean when it comes to romantic part-nerships? Given all the new tech tools at our disposal, we might assume our success and satisfaction rates are increasing expo-nentially. Technology gives us access to ever-widening yet hyper-specific dating pools—producing what we might call a surplus of "super daters." Take Nate Brewer,[4] a regular guy living in NYC. When it comes to dating, Nate knows what he wants. He's a rare breed: equal parts bookish academic and aspiring actor/model. He makes no apologies for the fact that he prefers—nay, demands—that his women be attractive, educated, petite, and hypersexual. His previous girlfriend was an Ivy-educated PhD student, and he expects that level of intellectual achievement in all his mates (and states as much in his online dating profiles). So, in his targeted searches, he filters for highly attractive women with a PhD who are slender and 5'4" or under—he also scans their profiles for clues that indicate a potentially high sex drive. And judging from his packed dating schedule, he has no problem finding women who match what he's looking for on paper.

In the last two decades, we've moved from a model of dating that required time to determine chemistry and compatibility to the "high-information relationship." That is to say, pre-Internet, con-texts and circumstances introduced you to a potential mate; once you demonstrated relative compatibility, the courtship period filled in the details. Now, over one-third of all new marriages start online—which means we first calculate personal data and professional stats, assuming that a comparable resume and self-reported keywords alone will equate with compatibility.[5] Is this inverse approach more or less stable? Is it more or less satisfying?

Knowing the minutiae of Nate's preferences—like whether he prefers burgers to pasta—should make getting into a relationship easier and more successful, right? Well, not if the dating sites and apps had their way. If ever there was an ironic threat to monogamy, it's our digital matchmakers, whose business model flourishes only if you're *unsuccessful* in finding a long-term mate, despite their alleged value proposition. Apps like Tinder serve up potential mates with the same abundance and velocity as our Chromecasts and Apple TVs do content—we can gorge on endless slideshows of potential mates while we binge-watch the new season of *House of Cards*. It's both efficiency and gluttony at its best. No one is waiting for serendipity to strike anymore. Is technology bad for relationships and great for dating? Have we all become professional daters?

Maybe we just need to redefine that term. I once went out with a guy who said something I've never forgotten: "A real dater—a professional dater—aims to date themselves right out of a job. If you're serious about dating, you hope that every date is your last."

This is an interesting concept: the notion of a "last date." Aisles full of bridal magazines and reality TV shows like *Say Yes to the Dress* confirm that most of us would still like to have a last date. But there is a disconnect. At our new all-you-can-eat dating buffet, we all can be Nate Brewers, hand-selecting the exact variety of partner we're in the market for ("I'll have a tall, dirty-blonde architect who loves large dogs, does triathlons, and lives below 14th St., please!"). But what is our goal in these relationships? Our appetite for the small stuff—that day-to-day grind that's so crucial to successful partnerships of any kind—has been dulled by the sheer human abundance presented to us. Individuals whose company we'd normally savor and focus on long enough to form a connection lose their appeal when dropped into a boundless sea of other options. We've adopted a "more is more" mindset, which often leaves us more bloated than satiated.

If marriage once offered the only reliable access to sex, and that's now available almost immediately in most dating circumstances, what is it we seek from these partnerships? How are those expectations communicated and negotiated? And what of accountability?

Mark Stein,[6] another regular guy, forgot to get married. After attending college on the East Coast, Mark moved to California and spent most of his twenties there, trying his hand as a screenwriter. In his thirties, he moved back to his hometown in Canada to care for his ailing parents and sort out their finances. He took over the family business, cashed out, and once his parents were healthy enough to care for themselves again, moved to New York City. Then he realized he was 42, and while he was financially set and already semi-retired, he was without the wife and kids he'd always imagined he'd have. Somehow that part of his life plan had slipped through the cracks, so he decided it was time to get down to business.

Mark knew that New York was *the* place to be to meet the kind of woman he wanted: smart (bordering on nerdy), cultured, preferably Jewish, and, if at all possible, a Tina Fey lookalike. Wide-eyed and giddily optimistic, Mark first tried online dating but was quickly discouraged. Despite his financial security, his advertised occupation was "writer," and since he had no real commercial success in that area, many women assumed he was essentially unemployed. His secret millionaire status, coupled with his 5'8" pudgy frame and misguided fashion sense, made for a frustratingly ineffective profile, despite his persistent, articulate attempts to make a genuine connection.

Around the same time he had lunch with a female friend from college. While they were eating, a woman at a neighboring table interrupted to ask a question, and within seconds the two women fell into an extended, intimate conversation. Mark had an epiphany: his attempts to meet women socially repeatedly failed, but in the presence of another woman, a female friend, initiating an exchange became infinitely easier. He hypothesized that he would be less threatening and more attractive to these potential mates in the company of another woman. What he needed was a wingwoman.

And so, Mark harnessed the power of technology in a different way—not by creating yet another online dating profile, but by placing the best Craigslist ad ever (really—it even made the coveted "Best of Craigslist" list, the reader-nominated list of unbelievable and amazing posts). He described his situation and goals and, miraculously, without seeming creepy or crazy, communicated what he wanted to do: hire a rotating bevy of wingwomen to attend wine tasting events, hang out in bookstores, and roam street festivals with him. And given the fact that it was 2008 and unemployment rates were soaring, he received hundreds of responses from bright, beautiful, outgoing women—none of whom wanted to be his future wife, but all of whom wanted to get paid to hang out with him and help him talk to other women.

I was one of the women who responded to Mark's ad—only I wasn't interested in being his wingwoman. Instead, I became his personal life coach and sociologist, working with him to upgrade his image, strategically execute each outing, and dissect each social exchange, all in the name of optimizing his delivery and finding him a mate. In other words, we transformed Mark's search for love into a startup.

The wingwoman experiment continued for several months, but despite impressive collective effort, it didn't yield many first dates. Mark and his hired guns had great luck when it came to meeting the most interesting woman in the room and talking to her for hours, but when it came time to get the number and "close the deal," he was already firmly parked in the friend zone. It was time to revise the strategy yet again.

Pickup artists (or PUAs) are an often unpopular group of men who specialize in "picking up" women. These dating gurus describe the men who just "get it" when it comes to how to approach, impress, and woo a woman as "naturals"—but thanks to technology, even those naturals are becoming endangered species. Once upon a time, we had no choice but to operate in physical networks of people, meeting and socializing with friends and friends of friends, some of whom became romantic partners. Online dating, on the other hand, demands a cold approach all the time—and cold approaches are difficult, even for naturals.

A longtime follower of the pickup artist community, Mark decided to investigate its newest evolution: not the tricks-and-lies approach described in Neil Strauss's *The Game*,[7] but rather a different breed of PUAs (they often prefer the term "dating coach," though the exact distinction is debatable), who use compliments and flattery to seduce women into . . . having a relationship with them. Sure, they might also date and sleep with a few women along the way, but for most, finding a long-term partner is often the goal—they just need some help with the execution.

Mark began attending countless weekend PUA seminars and worked with a dedicated dating coach to refine his "day game" and meet women (on his own) when they least expected it—on the subway, in Whole Foods, in the travel section of the Strand. He even started hosting couchsurfing potlucks—events he created for travelers and their hosts within the couchsurfing community—at the large apartment he was subletting to increase his exposure to potential mates.

And, sure enough, his efforts finally paid off. He is now married to a nice, nerdy woman with Tina Fey glasses. While won over via tactics he learned from his crew of helpers—from wingwomen to dating coaches to pickup artists to me, his wife feels more flatteringly wooed than deceptively hoodwinked. He didn't "trick" her into having a relationship with him; rather, he merely refined his dating skillset and upgraded the "product" on offer to her. A win-win situation.

Sure, by widening his net, Mark was ultimately playing a numbers game. But we could argue that mating has always been a numbers game, only the numbers now are of epic proportions. PUAs (of both the old and new persuasions) merely understand the numbers and look to defy them by approaching women very directly, in multiples, where there's less competition. And, unlike other more cavalier daters, these professionals and their committed students do their homework. They understand that if you mimic your date's language style, your date is 33 percent more likely to want to see you again[8]; they know that research shows that visual differentiation demonstrates status and competency, so they find a way to "peacock" and stand out in their appearance.[9] Some of these pickup gurus boast several million followers and tens of millions of dollars in annual profits from their work. They are not just the weird, sleazy guys on the fringes of society; they are savvy entrepreneurs, and more than a few people are paying attention.

So what's their hook? Not only are pickup artists analog in a digital world, but they fill an underserved niche in what they sell and how they sell it: namely, romance and the return of the alpha male. These men and their disciples are not necessarily the handsomest, most chiseled overachievers in the room. But that's not their appeal. Rather, they are direct, complimentary, and operate in the real world, not hidden behind a screen. Yes, there are some who are still just trolling for sex and behaving badly, but many of the men who pay high fees to attend dating seminars and hire coaches are nice, average guys looking for relationships—just like Mark.

Paul Janka is an attractive, Harvard-educated 40-year-old entrepreneur—and one of the most notorious pickup artists of the last decade: *The New York Observer* calls him "New York's PUA poster boy."[10] (Though he's not a perpetual playboy: Janka recently tied the knot with his longtime girlfriend, someone he picked up while following his own advice to "judge a woman based on how she behaves, not how she looks."[11]) Janka believes that most men currently lack the skills or emotional ability to connect with a woman—particularly strangers—face-to-face.[12] So how can they bridge this gap?

"We need help from professionals," argues self-proclaimed professional wingman Thomas Edwards.[13] "Most of the things we do we were taught by someone. Dating and relationships are no exception." Evan Katz, a dating coach who got his start writing online dating profiles, espouses the same logic: "Dating coaches are just specialists, like plumbers or personal trainers. They know their subject matter really well, to help you navigate an area of life that's really important, but often neglected. A lot of people are embarrassed to hire someone because they think they should just know, but they'll hire a contractor to build their cabinets, no problem."[14]

PUAs and dating coaches focus on in-person socialization. This is important, because technology doesn't just disrupt how we meet: it's also a physical buffer that deflects advances in public. When we arrive at a destination, we often divert our gaze immediately toward our phones—thereby blocking ourselves from potential social encounters. "Imagine if a guy saw that and approached her anyway," Edwards prompts. "It can be a refreshing conversation."

Evan Katz works primarily with what he describes as "highly functional women" in their mid-thirties to mid-fifties who just can't seem to find a guy who treats them well. One of Katz's central messages to women is that they are the CEOs of their own love lives, while the guy is just an intern applying for a job. He preaches the traditional PUA philosophy with a reverse-gender spin: You're in charge and you're the prize. They can either realize it, or you'll move on.

I'm not saying you have to go out and hire a pickup artist or a dating coach, but taking a more proactive, calculated approach to achieving your romantic goals is far more satisfying than passively waiting for something to happen. You set goals, analyze metrics, and invest in personal development in other aspects of your life—why would your love life be an exception?

The Love Santa

Romantic comedies are our modern-day fairy tales, and they center on the search for our one and only true love. In the easily forgotten 2001 movie *Kate and Leopold,* Leopold (Hugh Jackman), a duke, travels from the nineteenth century to the twenty-first and meets Kate (Meg Ryan—who else?). At one point Leopold serves Kate a candlelight dinner on the roof (to which he invited her via formal letter, obviously). Like a true rom-com female protagonist, Kate is traditionally unlucky in love. "I'm not very good with men," she says after making some sort of insulting comment to him mid-dinner.

"Perhaps you haven't found the right one?" Leopold responds, ever the gentleman. "Maybe," she says. "Or maybe the whole love thing is just a grown-up version of Santa Claus. Just a myth we've been fed since childhood. So we keep buying magazines and joining clubs and doing therapy and watching movies with hip-hop songs played over love montages, all in this pathetic attempt to explain why our Love Santa keeps getting caught in the chimney."[15]

The Love Santa. A terrific little gift of Hollywood nomenclature. Indeed, we are fed this fairy tale of a prince or princess—or a nineteenth-century duke, as the case may be—who will eventually sweep us off our feet, *if* we do everything right (look right, act right, follow all the right dating rules). And so we obsessively groom and self-analyze, and we read about new and improved ways to groom and self-analyze, ad infinitum. Only Love Santa never arrives. In other words, you've put out the push-up bra cookies to lure him in, and you wait and you wait, until finally you just have to put on your sweatpants and go to bed, resigned to the fact that Love Santa's not coming down your chimney tonight or any night. The search for The One—and the subsequent realization that it doesn't exist—is the adult equivalent of learning that there's no Santa Claus.

Think that sort of fanciful thinking is relegated to movie nonsense or childhood myths? Think again. Seventy-four percent of Americans believe there is one true soul mate with whom they are destined to be—and perhaps even more surprising, this number is highest amongst men (74 percent of men; 71 percent of women).[16] This romantic ideal ultimately hinders, not helps, the quest for long-term connection: individuals who adhere to the soul mate fantasy demonstrate lower frequencies of commitment when their actual relationship—inevitably—doesn't operate perfectly and conflict arises.[17]

So what's the alternative to chasing The One?

A few years ago, Maya,[18] a 31-year-old East Coast native, was working at a big law firm in New York City—and hating every minute of it. That spring, she took some vacation time and visited a friend in Argentina. Her friend's friend, David,[19] also a 31-year-old lawyer, was in Argentina as well. He was equally disenchanted with his law job in his hometown of San Francisco and was taking some time to reassess. The two quickly fell into a fun vacation romance that Maya assumed would end when she returned to New York. They remained in contact over the summer, and when he returned to the States in the fall, they planned to meet in New York and perhaps rekindle the fire. Over the course of the next six weeks, they spent as much time as possible together and fell completely, head-over-heels in love. They decided to quit their jobs—officially, this time—and take several months to travel together. Upon their return, Maya relocated to San Francisco, they moved in together, and each started their own private practices. They married the next year and remain happily together.

I don't tell you this story to encourage you to quit your job and flee to South America. (Though if you do, please let me know how it turns out!) I share this story because, as soul-matey as their story might sound, there's another way of reading it. Maya believes that a lasting relationship requires two things: a feeling and a choice. We all know that "feeling"—some call it a spark, some call it chemistry—but either way, it's a "know it when you find it" sort of thing. That's not to say you can only have that feeling with one person. In fact, it's precisely because you *can* experience it multiple times that the success of any relationship depends on the second half of the equation: making a choice. That is to say, accepting the challenge of not moving on to another exciting new option as soon as complexity and conflict arise. It's the more practical—yet still romantic—antidote to what I refer to as Soul Mate Syndrome, or the perpetual search for the Love Santa.

A feeling and a choice. Could it be that simple? Feeling the spark is the easy part. The real challenge lies in committing to making that choice again, every day, for decades—even when the spark flickers, rather than engaging in relationship Chatroulette.

Mihaly Csikszentmihalyi, the leading researcher on positive psychology, argues that people experience the most satisfying kind of happiness when they are in a state of "flow." In *Flow: The Psychology of Optimal Experience*, he speaks to the particular challenge of long-term relationships:

> How to keep love fresh? The answer is the same as it is for any other activity. To be enjoyable, a relationship must become more complex. To become more complex, the partners must discover new potentialities in themselves and in each other. To discover these, they must invest attention in each other . . . This in itself is a never-ending process, a lifetime's task.[20]

Some cynics might see a lasting relationship as the equivalent of a tech "unicorn"—the designation given to the few companies whose valuation exceeds $1 billion. Unicorns are generally elusive and unrealistic—a pipedream for most VCs. And yet, stories like Mark Stein's and Maya and David's abound. Most people, including me, still subscribe to the idea that life is simply better with companionship, no matter how hard to find and harder to define the relationship may be. In Elizabeth Gilbert's book *Committed,* one of the characters comments, "Sometimes life is too hard to be alone, and sometimes life is too good to be alone."[21] Today's complex dating scene can sometimes feel discouraging and, despite the abundance of options and freedoms, companionship may feel perpetually out of reach. But as the poet Criss Jami writes, "To say that one waits a lifetime for his soulmate to come around is a paradox. People eventually get sick of waiting, take a chance on someone, and by the art of commitment become soulmates, which takes a lifetime to perfect."[22]

To quote another great love poet, former Secretary of Defense Donald Rumsfeld, the "unknown unknowns" are relatively few and far between when it comes to dating in our techno-charged information era. But the opportunity to rethink how and to whom you're committed, to redefine your relationship role, and to create your own personal love story has never been greater. But after years of dedicating yourself to blind dates, matchmaking intros, endless online first dates, and the occasional, serendipitous meet-cute, it's easy to grow weary. And so, many opt out of relationships and even sex altogether, fatigued from the abundance of choice and an anything-goes rulebook. Our modern dating and mating configurations—Craigslist missed connections, *Second Life* marriages, pickup artist seminars—likely won't match that of our parents or our children. But partnerships, however undefined and unprecedented they may be, still happen and still matter more than ever. The fairy tale has been disrupted, and while it may not be a neat and tidy "happily ever after," we're definitely not screwed.

SCRUM MASTER CHEAT SHEET

Can you rise above our culture of perpetual nexting and have the patience to cultivate relationship complexity and flow? Here's how to make your quest a little smarter and a lot less frustrating.

☞ **DON'T GO IT ALONE.** No startup operates in isolation. And neither do you. You construct your life in concert with others. Friends and clients may turn into business partners. Acquaintances may become gateways to new potential collaborations or introductions.

And friends of friends become spouses and life partners. But before you can meaningfully connect and explore the possibilities of these relationships, you need to buy into the fact that partnerships—even when imperfect—make you stronger and your life better. Former Disney CEO Michael Eisner argues on behalf of partnerships for personal success: "Many people you think are individual achievers, in fact have either a strong spousal partner over many years or a business partner who's either in the background, not given enough publicity, or less egocentric."[23] More often than not, our output—and our happiness—wanes when we isolate. But that's not to say you should latch onto anyone who bats an eye at you. Author and motivational speaker Jim Rohn urged people to choose their companions wisely, arguing that we are the average of the five people we spend the most time with, meaning connection can be as much of a downfall as a key ingredient to success. And as we've already established, living a networked life now means committing to both in-person relationships as well as mindful, technology-assisted interactions.

☞ **BEEF UP YOUR SOFT SKILLS.** In a *New York Times* interview with Gary Smith, the CEO of telecommunications company Cicna, he emphasizes the value of "soft skills": "Relationships really matter, and you need to get that right, both for your career as an individual and as a future leader. I think a lot of people pay attention to the technical stuff and the hard stuff. But it's the softer side that will get you every time if you're not paying attention to it. It's probably the biggest determinant of whether you're going to be successful."[24] We most often use the term "soft skills" in relationship to emotional intelligence, or EQ. These skills are the social graces and interpersonal skills that are less easily defined or quantified than hard skills, but which often factor as key differentiators.

Author and scholar Arthur C. Brooks argues on behalf of "romantic entrepreneurialism," defined as the deliberate cultivation of two key entrepreneurial qualities: courage and mindfulness.[25] Fear, he explains, is contradictory to love—and therefore love demands courage. His call for mindfulness is akin to Csikszentmihalyi's recipe for flow—both demand a commitment to presence for the cultivation of connection. Soft skills figure prominently in the business of relationships.

Relationships, like career paths, don't fit into a perfect mold. They aren't always predictable and "safety" is largely an illusion. Risk abounds. Planning is for naught. And failure—to varying degrees—is imminent along the way. You can, however, redefine "success" and rewrite your own rules of engagement, but not just through ticking boxes and downloading apps. Be bold. Be present. And feel the difference.

☛ HAVE A FEELING, MAKE A CHOICE. In our quest to connect, vulnerabilities and second guesses abound, which can undermine the courage we need to dive in. And while you can't always plan ahead, you can come to terms with how you want to conduct your relationship startups.

True love, soul mates—whether you're a "believer" or not, all potential mates are not created equal. Too often we think in extremes: destiny or practicality. But the feeling/choice formula allows for a little of both. What are your non-negotiables? Aside from those, throw out the checklist and check back in with the feeling side of the equation. This isn't an attempt to oversimplify a complex question, but reverting back to the basics of how you feel and what you need is the simplest way to keep moving forward. Consider it your relationship MVP: sometimes you need to strip away the noise to understand the core value proposition. And that makes committing to a choice that much easier.

THE LAZY LOWDOWN: TOP TEN CHAPTER TAKEAWAYS

1. Partnerships are hard. Just like everything else of value.
2. Sometimes life is like a Third World prison. Are you in the right company?
3. Baggage can strengthen a partnership, not just weigh it down.
4. Go rogue: be a relationship entrepreneur.
5. Approach your love life like your plumbing: enlist professional help as needed.
6. Ditch Love Santa. He's a bloated disappointment.
7. A spark can become a flame if you keep saying yes.
8. You're as good as the company you keep. Choose wisely.
9. Find flow through complexity and depth—not relationship Chatroulette.
10. Fear squashes love. Be brave, be bold.

10.

Bellyflop with Grace

THE ART OF FAILURE

Failure is the opportunity to begin again more intelligently.
—HENRY FORD, *My Life and Work*

In 2003, Niklas, along with two friends from Helsinki, competed in a mobile gaming competition and won. That victory led Niklas to launch his own company, which eventually became known as Rovio Entertainment. Over the next five years, Rovio developed a whopping 51 games, some of which did very well, but none of which were an obvious, huge success. Struggling to stay afloat, the company was on the brink of bankruptcy when Apple launched its app store and iOS platform in 2008. This new iPhone technology marked a significant turning point in the accessibility of consumer gaming, allowing developers to sell to millions of people via one company. And it was a saving grace for Rovio, who was in desperate need of a big hit. Niklas and his team shuffled through hundreds of new game ideas, but they never could have planned for what happened next.

Shortly after the app store launch, Rovio switched to the iPhone as its development platform and released a game called Angry Birds. It wasn't just another game, however. Rovio had done its homework. Over the years, it ran ongoing focus groups and accumulated knowledge about what challenged and pleased gamers. They also understood the demographics and behavior patterns of iPhone users—many of whom were not dedicated gamers—and designed the game accordingly, making it simple enough for the layperson but challenging enough to capture even hard-core gamers. As a result, a wide breadth of people eagerly took to Angry Birds.

And yet, Angry Birds still wasn't an overnight global sensation. It first topped the app charts in Rovio's native Finland, then crept into other smaller markets, gradually gaining popularity in large markets like the United States. Three years later, Angry Birds reached over 1 billion downloads.[1]

And while 1 billion downloads may seem like a huge victory—which it was—it came only after many, many relative failures. When on the brink of bankruptcy after producing dozens of forgettable games, instead of closing up shop, Niklas Hed pressed on one last time. And it was that final attempt—his fifty-second—that produced the most downloaded game of all time.

Regardless of how you measure it, success doesn't always (or usually) happen right off the bat. We see this again and again in the startup world. It's often the second, third—or in the case of Rovio Entertainment, fifty-second—attempt that is the home run.

And while it may not take you quite that long to get it right, rest assured you're in good company if it does. As the writer J. M.

Barrie said, "Life is a long lesson in humility."[2] Once you give yourself permission to fall down regularly, the journey becomes a lot less grueling and far more fun. Every failed attempt, you'll find, is an opportunity for growth. And it's actually the failures that pave the road to eventual success. But how? Is it simply that 51 wrongs make a right?

We're often told that timing is everything. Many startups explain their failures as a result of bad timing. *Too early, too late—we were doomed from the start!* But not everyone buys it. Dave McClure, investor and founder of 500 Startups, a Silicon Valley accelerator, rejects this explanation as a convenient excuse. Instead, he (bluntly) argues, the culprit is some combination of not enough effort and just selling the wrong thing: "Startups don't fail because of 'bad timing'—they fail because people don't get shit done, because no customers want to buy their crap, or because the competition beats the crap out of everyone else. Telling yourself it was just 'bad timing' is almost always a self-indulgent exercise in rationalization. (now STFU and get back to work.)"[3] Sure, there are times when certain ventures are more challenging to get off the ground (like, say, selling luxury services during an economic downturn), but McClure's logic dictates there's a right product and a right approach for every environment. You just need to find it. And keep working until you do. But this is hardly a new school of thought.

Henry Ford was obsessed with the automobile. Determined to improve on its earliest iterations, he began tinkering with a new prototype—but first found a series of false starts. His eventual prototype was impressive enough to earn him venture backing, but when he failed to scale production as planned, investors abandoned him. Like a true entrepreneur, he took that setback as an opportunity for learning and analyzed what went wrong before diving back in.

Anyone else would have taken that series of events as an insurmountable setback, but Ford championed the education it gave him. And after refining and reworking his production model, he linked up with a new partner and personally guided each step of the manufacturing process until he got it right. Against staggering odds, after having already lost the faith of his backers, Henry Ford finally created an affordable automobile for the masses—and became one of the richest men alive.[4]

Like his contemporary Thomas Edison, Ford did not invent something completely new. The automobile already existed, as did the lightbulb. And like Edison, Ford did not score a win on the first try, or even the fifth. What Edison teaches us about experimentation, Ford exemplifies with regard to abject failure. Edison is credited with saying that "many of life's failures are people who didn't realize how close they were to success when they gave up." They were on their fifty-first try. If they only knew what awaited with the fifty-second.

We are told that patience is a virtue, but we struggle more than ever to achieve and maintain it. Contemporary culture is all about instant gratification. Audible pings notify us in real time of messages, status updates, and current events. Minimizing wait-time in all areas of life is the raison d'être of many up-and-coming startups. We order everything from food to flowers to household goods for delivery on demand. We can watch what we want, when we want it. Technology, it seems, has rendered patience an antiquated virtue.

We've also lost patience with cultivating success, despite the fact that the slow build is still very much how the world works. Yes, a few companies like Instagram achieve nearly overnight success, but that is not the entrepreneurial (or human) norm—and certainly not one that can be easily or realistically replicated. But when those are the stories dominating the news, it's easy to forget that they are the exception—everyone else is Angry Birds and Henry Ford. And this is good news. Because having the right idea in the right place at the right time with the right team on your first try—the entrepreneurial equivalent of winning the lottery—is a dauntingly unrealistic standard.

Sometimes companies fail not because they lack a stellar team and a great idea, or even the right timing, but because VCs fail to recognize the project's potential. Investors are human and make mistakes, and successful investing is anything but an exact science. Some of the most highly valued companies were once in this camp. The members of one prominent venture capital firm, Bessemer Venture Partners, publicly highlight the companies they wish they'd invested in when they had the chance—what they call their "anti-portfolio."[5] They said no to HP, Apple, eBay, Facebook, Google, PayPal, and many other massively successful companies. Their response to the eBay pitch: "Stamps? Coins? Comic books? You've *got* to be kidding. No-brainer pass."

Perhaps you've had similar regrets at different times in your life. You did everything right, and yet, life didn't feel like a "win"—you look back and wonder what went wrong. Happily, in Silicon Valley, failing is common and respected enough to be a badge of honor—as long as you grow from it. There's even a conference for startup founders called FailCon, where entrepreneurs talk about what went wrong, what they learned, and how they eventually transformed that failure into success. Unlike other professional sectors, failure is paraded proudly among peers in the startup community.

San Francisco hosts a lot of conferences in addition to Fail-Con. A lot. From small maker fairs to the 150,000-plus-person behemoth that is Salesforce's Dreamforce conference, people flock to the Bay Area for professional events all year, every year. Hotel rates surge during peak times, and during the 2015

Dreamforce event alone, the hotels not only filled up, but the giant cruise ship hired by Salesforce also maxed out. (Salesforce is another company nearly every investor in Silicon Valley regrets passing on.)

Eight years prior to that Dreamforce event, in 2007, designers Brian Chesky and Joe Gebbia saw how impacted San Francisco was during these big conferences and looked at it as an opportunity. These financially flailing roommates launched a service whereby they hosted conference goers in their apartment—on air beds—and fed them a home-cooked breakfast. They called it AirBed & Breakfast, and a business was born.

The following year they brought on a technical cofounder, Nathan Blecharczyk, to help expand their site and round out their team, but investors gave them the same dead-end response: "The market is too small." Investors and friends alike thought it was an absurd idea. And even they weren't initially sure it had legs. But they pressed on.

In 2008 there was another hotel shortage—this time at the Democratic National Convention in Denver. They launched their website with 800 listings two weeks before the convention. Still desperate for money, they also launched a separate venture simultaneously, selling cereal. But not just any cereal: "Obama O's" and "Cap'n McCains." To be clear, this wasn't some large-scale, sophisticated manufacturing operation. No, the resourceful entrepreneurs created these $40-per-box, 500-run limited edition political breakfast treats with glue guns and cardboard. And yet, the cereal earned them real cash while also serving as a marketing tool during the convention. They donated 5 percent of profits to the respective campaigns and made tens of thousands of dollars in the process, while serving up a compelling story for bloggers and media outlets, putting AirBed & Breakfast on the public map.[6]

In 2009, they interviewed for Y Combinator, a startup accelerator that incubates companies and gives them a small cash infusion in exchange for a cut of the company. The AirBed & Breakfast team recalls not doing well in the interview—until they presented the Y Combinator founder, Paul Graham, with a box of Obama O's. Graham was impressed by the scrappiness with which the founders were funding their company and admitted them into the group. Not because he was sold on their idea per se, but because he believed in them.[7]

This happens again and again in the startup world: VCs are unsure of the idea, but they see a spark in the founders. Something that demonstrates they're bound to succeed, even if it takes them a while to get it right. So they bet on the people and accept that they'll miss a few shots, while knowing that the resilient types will emerge that much stronger—and probably, eventually, victorious.

In this case, Paul Graham was right. Brian Chesky, Joe Gebbia, and Nathan Blecharczyk took AirBed & Breakfast and turned it into Airbnb, a company now valued at over $25 billion.[8]

Lest you think my life is a long series of wins, I assure you I've had plenty of my own 51-failures days. When I first dipped my toe in the startup world, it was a complete accident. One night, after a few drinks at a friend's house party, I joked about an idea I had for a new social media platform: a spin-off of Friendster, one of the original social platforms—only this one tracked your dating network, indicating everyone you've dated and everyone they've dated, thereby visualizing your larger social network via your dating history. Someone in the group thought I was serious and told our other mutual friend, who was a computer programmer. The idea was admittedly terrible, but once we started discussing it, we isolated the element that wasn't so embarrassingly horrible: the desire to track meaningful, in-person communication. This was back before Facebook took off, when MySpace still dominated. So we ditched the dating component and attempted to build a marketing strategy around the MySpace model, but nothing seemed to stick. And since we were both busy with other projects, we shelved it. Then, a few years later, the timing felt better—both personally and across the industry. Social media was exploding, and the ideas we'd discussed suddenly seemed more viable. So we officially launched Splice, a platform for tracking connections, with the intention of raising venture capital.

After pitches at Meetup groups and multiple exploratory meetings with investors (all of which ended with a polite "come back to us when you've got some traction"), we thought of another path: shifting from a consumer product to an enterprise focus, with an emphasis on finding opportunities for knowledge-sharing and connection internally within large organizations. So we brought on another partner with enterprise expertise, joined forces with the likes of IBM, were accepted into a tech incubator, and dove headfirst into fundraising in multiple cities with every investor who would see us.

But the money never came. We needed customers before we could secure investment, and before we could get customers we needed a working prototype. And since that prototype required hiring an additional programmer with a different skillset, we reached a stalemate. There are a hundred different ways we could have made this work, but the partnerships were crumbling and the switch to enterprise pushed the company well beyond our technical expertise, leaving the whole thing flailing and unfundable.

After 18 months of working on the project—without compensation—I had no money, no company, and no idea what to do next. It was a personal low. I had hit rock bottom. I borrowed money from friends to pay my rent that month and burst into tears nearly every day for the two weeks that followed. Then, amid the wallowing, I had an epiphany.

While I was busy hustling to raise money for Splice, the investors looking at my bio kept saying the same thing: "Tell us more about your other company. The intelligent image consulting. That sounds interesting. Why don't you scale that?" Their advice evaded me while on the money trail for the other project, and it wasn't until Splice bellyflopped that I was able to open my mind to the opportunity that had been in front of me all along. So after everything else crumbled, I shifted focus out of desperation—and it set me on a path that completely changed the course of my life.

I put away the Kleenex, and reached out to everyone I knew who seemed remotely relevant to the new venture. For several weeks, I had coffee meetings with friends and friends of friends, bending their ears, parsing out the good advice from the bad, and gradually piecing together a plan to formally scale a company I'd previously dismissed as a side hobby. And two weeks later, with a new business partner and a team of former students, I launched.

I still didn't have funding, and the new venture still needed validation, but my spirit and sense of purpose were renewed. In a matter of days, I went from feeling defeated to believing I was on the rise. Some might call that delusion. But failures and wins can be hard to differentiate. What felt like a devastating defeat was really paving the foundation for something different—something that was a better fit for me and that made perfect sense once I embarked on it, but which never occurred to me until it was the only thing left standing. It's amazing how incapacitated we become when we narrow our outlets for success.

That initial moment of defeat, when I had to explain to everyone I'd encountered for the last year and a half that Splice no longer existed and wasn't ever going to (at least not on my watch), was embarrassing. And humbling. And I was exhausted. I wanted to curl up in a ball and hope it would pass and that something new would fall at my feet. But running away wasn't a viable option. And the something new I longed for had been there all along. I just had to open my eyes to it.

These sorts of serial failures before a win are not exclusive to the startup world. Susan Lucci played villain Erica Kane on daytime soap opera *All My Children* from its debut in 1970 until its final episode in 2011. In 1991, she was reportedly the highest paid female actress on television, earning $1 million per year.[9] And yet, she was not formally recognized for her success. Between 1978 and 1998 she was nominated for an Emmy award for Outstanding Lead Actress in a Drama Series 18 times without a single win. Her repeated losses were parodied on *Saturday Night Live,* and she even hosted the awards show during her losing streak.[10] Despite her popularity and bankability, she didn't take home a golden statue until 1999—her nineteenth nomination.

More recently, actor Jon Hamm was nominated for an Emmy 15 times before he finally won, and Amy Poehler has yet to take home an award after 16 nominations. Making lemonade out of lemons, the two once banded together to throw a "losers" after-party—referred to as the "Losers' Lounge." Entry to the party required Emmy winners to leave their awards at the door and donate to a charity of Hamm and Poehler's choosing—proving that even defeat can be hip.[11]

And failure certainly isn't relegated to our careers. Zsa Zsa Gabor is perhaps best known not for her acting but for her nine marriages—the last of which, with a man 26 years her junior, has gone on for 30 years.

So what might it mean to fail? Is it about the total number of nominations or just the eventual win? The marriages that ended or the one that finally endured? We are often quick to label an outcome or person as a failure, and yet, for scrappy entrepreneurs and villainous soap stars alike, it's a murky category. Looked at pessimistically, the total possible ways in which we might fail are endless: from divorce to bankruptcy, and from getting laid off to receiving a rejection letter from your dream school, there are opportunities to fail in every corner of every life stage. And it's not just the big stuff we can screw up. There's an equally abundant number of smaller failures that await, like a weekend of excess and bad decisions or a careless fender bender. Some—and possibly all—of these momentary setbacks will happen to all of us at one time or another. It's impossible to completely avoid them, nor should you. One relationship may end, and while it leaves you temporarily depressed, it may ultimately free you up to meet the person you will eventually marry. Or the loss of a job may force you to think about career options you never previously entertained. And that unexpected detour you took may actually be less of a time waster and more of what the late artist Bob Ross called a "happy accident," offering unanticipated treasures along the way.

And if the promise of failure still gets you down, focus instead on the potential comeback. The only thing people love more than the schadenfreude of other people's failure is the thrill of rooting for the underdog.

From my San Francisco apartment on the Embarcadero, I look out over the majestic San Francisco Bay—the mountains blurry on the horizon, several lush islands floating throughout, and a swirling of micro-climates and rapidly changing weather conditions that create a spectacular show of technicolor skylights at dawn and dusk. Most weekends are sunny and mild, and there's almost always a light breeze, so beginning early Friday afternoon, dozens of sailboats pop up from the Bay Bridge to the Golden Gate. It's a serene scene, the white sails floating by silently in the distance. But in September 2013, just one week before I moved in, those normally peaceful waters were tense with one of the most dramatic sporting competitions in history.

The America's Cup is not just another race. It is a business venture unto itself. Master sailors, cutting-edge technology, strategic calculations, and high-end sponsorship combine to make it as much a startup as a competition. The teams don't just hire a skipper; they're also led by a separate CEO. Some might argue the America's Cup, which dates back to 1851, is the Wild West of professional sporting competitions: very little regulation and a boatload of unpredictable variables. No wonder it's only held every three to five years.

Going into the 2013 America's Cup in San Francisco—the first and only time it's been held in the city by the bay—Oracle Team USA (owned by the illustrious Larry Ellison and performed on his $10 million state-of-the-art vessel[12]) was favored to win, despite having been dinged with a two-point cheating penalty during a warm-up event. The Americans needed to win 11 races to take the Cup, while Emirates Team New Zealand, their challenger, needed to win 9. But even with that disadvantage, Team USA's optimism did not wane.

The competition did not begin as planned. Team USA lost three of the first four races—winning race four by only eight seconds. With their confidence shaken, Ellison's crew asked for a postponement card to delay the next race for 48 hours. They used the time to make some adjustments, but still went on to lose races six and seven. Team USA had only 12 more chances to score ten more wins, while New Zealand was only three races away from victory. Things were not looking good.

In race eight, the Kiwis nearly capsized as Ellison's catamaran headed straight for them, and Team USA finally scored its second win. Race nine was a particularly miraculous victory: despite Team New Zealand's lead, the race was scratched due to a time limit cap, forcing a redo and giving Team USA another win. New Zealand went on to win the next two races, further cementing their lead. For Team USA, failure seemed imminent.

But then something nobody saw coming happened: Team USA hit its stride and won the next eight races in a row, miraculously beating Team New Zealand in the nineteenth race.

No one would have bet on the Americans mid-competition. The crowds—regardless of their country of origin—cheered on New Zealand. But as the tide began to turn, so did the audience's support. Team USA, against all odds and rational prediction, had done the impossible. On the brink of a blowout, they staged the greatest comeback in the history of the competition.

History is littered with examples of people and organizations that come from behind to narrowly skirt defeat. The triumphant tale of the 2013 America's Cup is in no way intended to slip you into an optimism bias coma. I don't want you to walk away thinking you are the statistical exception when it comes to failure. But failure, like success, operates on a pendulum. Failure and success are not absolute opposites—they coexist on a spectrum. They are complements. And sometimes they're even one and the same, when you shift perspective. Which means comebacks *can* happen. Failure *is* relative. And a loss—just like a win—can transform dramatically when the wind inevitably changes course.

SCRUM MASTER CHEAT SHEET

Rethink your relationship with failure—how you define it, and how you deal with it—and you may be surprised what it offers. Here's how to take back the power and make failure your bitch.

☞ **MAKE SPACE FOR FAILURE.** Decluttering is all the rage. Though hardly new, the art of purging and organizing has made an impressive comeback as the latest life-improvement It concept (witness Marie Kondo's bestseller, *The Life-Changing Magic of Tidying*

Up). Consciously letting go of things we don't need has long been recognized as therapeutic—cathartic, if you will. Discarding does more than merely remove unwanted stuff: it also makes room for more. More of what you love. More of what makes you happy. Or just more space to breathe. Failure is probably not on your list of things to fill that void. But maybe it should be.

By now you've (hopefully) embraced the merits of calculated risk taking. If you're not failing along the way, you're probably not risking enough. That means it's time to up the stakes. Tossing out the pressure to succeed at every turn frees you to play with possibilities. You can take comfort in the knowledge that an occasional flop doesn't permanently scar you so much as positively condition you. Making space for failure softens the blow of disappointment that will inevitably arrive. It doesn't make you a loser, and it shouldn't make you a quitter. But you need to make peace with your enemy before you can become allies.

☞ **TRANSCRIBE ADVERSITY.** A popular Silicon Valley mantra encourages you to "fail fast, fail often." If taken literally, that could be a reckless directive. But its underlying intention is to encourage you to learn quickly from past mistakes and leverage that knowledge to help strengthen your next endeavor. It means that the demise of one thing is the seed of the next. Growth, however, doesn't emerge simply as a result of failure.

The key to limiting your "Losers' Lounge" failure fiestas is active reflection. Jonathan Haidt, in *The Happiness Hypothesis*, speaks to the power of cultivating resilience.[13] The argument goes that you need to experience adversity to grow, and without hard-earned growth, you'll have little long-term happiness.

So how do you grow from adversity? It's not achieved passively—one does not grow merely by experiencing "bad" things. Nor is it achieved by quickly rushing into the next thing/person/project. Rather, it is through the deliberate processing of an event—the "sense-making," as Haidt refers to it. Haidt says this sense-making should be a written reflection of your thoughts, put down on paper just for you. External action and the constant articulation of our every thought and feeling is now a societal default. But we need to regularly retreat into reflection before we can act again from a place of strength. Studies show that writing about adversity is more than a Dear Diary pity party; it's a simple yet powerful method for growing stronger as a result of failure. James Pennebaker's research shows that people who write following a trauma visit the doctor fewer times the following year than those who don't.[14] Mindfully processing setbacks is a scientifically proven method for personal transformation and a healthier, happier life. So let the ink flow.

☞ **KNOW YOUR BREAKING POINT.** Lest you think I'm failure's cheerleader, allow me to clarify: Failure will happen. And it should. And it will suck. And the more you deny that fact, the less equipped you'll be to capitalize on the tough-love gifts it bears. But complacency is not the answer. Failure is not shrug-worthy. It's hard and humbling. And like heartbreak, the most recent time still stings as badly as the first time. But by developing a strategy for dealing with it, it won't knock the wind out of you quite so much, making getting back on track that much easier.

But how much failure is too much? It's important to know how much you can take before you start to truly lose hope. Resilience is a delicate balance between pushing beyond what's comfortable and yielding to your breaking point. Have reverence for your limits. Failure is a dance. Be sure you're leading.

THE LAZY LOWDOWN: TOP TEN CHAPTER TAKEAWAYS

1. Fifty-one wrongs don't always make a right. But they might.
2. Fall down, get dirty, stand back up. Repeat.
3. Failure is a mental bulldozer: It clears away the brush. Pay attention to what's left standing.
4. Give yourself permission to lose, and you acquire the ability to succeed.
5. Take it from Zsa Zsa: Sometimes life saves the best for last. Be patient. It's simple, darling.
6. You're the skipper of your own life. The winds will change, but you're driving the boat.
7. Fortune operates on a pendulum. Be the comeback kid.
8. Bob Ross was right: Mistakes can be happy accidents. Shift your perspective.
9. Fail better. Know your limits.
10. Own failure or it will own you.

11.

Peace Out and Level Up

The end is where we start from.

—T. S. Eliot, *Four Quartets*

Andrew, a quirky former music major with a love of comedy, knew that everyone loves a deal. But with so many bargains out there, you're bound to miss most of them. He had a thought: What if he could somehow transform how people find deals? So he launched a company built on the premise that businesses would be willing to give deep discounts if they could access a large, focused customer base. The bargains he negotiated ranged from 50 to 90 percent off the normal price, with a minimum number of individuals required to buy in for the deal to happen, and the stipulation that they use it within a specified time period. Adding to the excitement, access to the deals was only made available for a short time: you only had a small window to purchase the good or service. Offering daily deals for everything from dinner for two to laser hair removal, his company, ingeniously named Groupon, reinvented how the everyday person makes purchases—and, in return, how businesses attract new clients. It was novel and exciting and seemed to promise a way that everyone—the customer, the service provider, and Groupon—could win.

For a while, it worked. Less than two years after it launched, Groupon was valued at over a billion dollars, with a sales growth rate among the fastest in history.[1] Around that same time, rumors circulated that Yahoo offered a $3 billion buyout,[2] only to be topped by Google, who offered the daily deal site $6 billion, with a $700 million earnout—which would've made it Google's biggest acquisition to date.[3] But worried that antitrust concerns might scuttle the deal, and clinging to the belief that they could grow even bigger, Groupon declined Google's offer and instead went public, with *The Wall Street Journal* reporting that Andrew confidently declared, "Like, okay, we're the best company in the world."[4]

Two years later, in 2012, Andrew was dubbed "Worst CEO of the Year" by CNBC.[5] Groupon was hemorrhaging money and struggling to turn a profit as the novelty of the daily deal model wore thin. Participating companies grew disillusioned, as well, with few purchasers converting into regular customers. To top it off, Groupon's accounting practices were under scrutiny by regulators. Of the $946 million raised in 2010, $810 million went to Andrew and the original stakeholders, much of which was paid out just before the company filed its IPO paperwork—which, as Forbes put it, raised questions as to "who-knew-what-when."[6] And then in 2012, Groupon announced that it needed to revise its 2011 fourth-quarter numbers, raising some eyebrows.[7] Andrew

Mason was caught in a downward spiral, plummeting as quickly as he had risen. A few months later, he was pushed out of the company.

Groupon continues to operate, but given how everything played out after the acquisition offers, it's hard to imagine that there aren't a few regrets on the part of its management. Groupon simply lost its luster. It stopped being the startup darling that attracted top talent and instead became a media punching bag. It didn't "fail" by many standards, but things undoubtedly went downhill.

It's good to know when to call it a day. I'm not talking about your death or about your "Irish exit" from Saturday's party. I'm talking about the ability to recognize when it's time to celebrate a milestone and start the process over again. That moment when it's time to wrap up the current situation and start daydreaming about the next one. Because before you can start something new, you need to tie up loose ends. And recognizing that moment isn't always easy or obvious.

Exits. We make a lot of them in our lives. Some more graciously than others. Some voluntary, some forced. And some of bigger consequence than others. In the startup world, exits are the mythical endgame. That thing entrepreneurs dream of. The BIG exit, to be more precise. Remember the "unicorns" I mentioned? The startups valued (pre-exit) at $1 billion or more? As of 2015, only around 143 companies qualified for this elite designation.[8] Most entrepreneurs want to be one, and all investors want to spot one—when they're still small and unrecognizable as such. Groupon was once a unicorn. But is betting on bigger always better?

Sometimes companies exit because they're acquired for a lot of money. Other times it's a sort of flash sale—things aren't going well and they just want out, so they join forces with a bigger company and broker a talent acquisition, or take a smaller cash payout and move on. Either way, it can be hard to place a numeric value on something you've worked so hard on, and it can be hard to give up the quest to make it bigger and better, which leads some entrepreneurs to hang on too long.

It's quintessentially human to wait too long. At times, it's even beneficial. It can take a while for some things to blossom. But more often, the writing's on the wall, yet we refuse to admit defeat.

Why do we cling when we know we shouldn't? What keeps us from moving forward? Often our stasis is a byproduct of fear. Fear of being alone, fear of failure. Maybe it's an attempt to avoid change, or just a fear of being publicly humiliated if our desired outcome doesn't unfold as planned. New research shows that we stay in suboptimal relationships or settle for not getting what we need or want from our partners because the fear of being single trumps the discontent, to an astonishing degree.[9] The fear of loneliness is paralyzing. So, too, is changing jobs, so we often choose to stay in an uninspired or miserable position, comforted by familiarity that breeds a false sense of security, despite our misery. We fear the general unknown perhaps even more than loneliness. And so we choose guaranteed *un*happiness over potential flourishing—because it seems easier at the time.

In fact, it's far worse than just complacency. We go to great lengths to fend off change. Why? Because you might say that our brains become addicted to the status quo. We may tell ourselves we're just waiting for the right moment to make our move. But, as we'll explore in the next chapter, waiting for perfect timing often leads to more delays, because once that new mini-milestone arrives, there are new circumstances to deal with, any of which might shift the status quo and "sabotage" the timing yet again. Procrastination will always prevail—if you let it.

To be sure, exits are a double-edged sword. On one hand, they're thrillingly laced with possibility. On the other, there's a ripple effect of adjustments that demand your attention. "Negative" change—a death, the loss of a job, the undesired end to a relationship—may usher in possibilities you never imagined, yet you may not be in the right frame of mind to take advantage of them. And even when it's positive on the surface—a promotion, a new home—change still brings plenty of stress with it (now you have to learn your new job or fill your new home with furniture), leaving us uneasy. New knowledge to acquire, new routines to master, a general disruption to a life that's largely been on autopilot: as illogical as it may sound, we fear success as much as we fear failure—because success is definitively coupled with change. And change is hard.

So what should you do instead of waiting for the universe to act on your behalf?

Keeping your mind ripe and ready for change is the first step. But you have to train it, because it will resist. Don't let change be something that happens to you—make it something you inflict upon yourself regularly. And while that might seem scary, overcoming that fear again and again—not just when catastrophe strikes, but in your everyday life—will enhance your happiness. It's the thoughtful ritualization of change, and a reverence for how we deal with it and what it does to us, that generates the greatest rewards.

Be the Boss of Change

We joke about growing pains, but to a certain extent, the process of self-discovery never ends. And there's rarely a road map for whatever stage you're in. When companies are acquired, there's media buzz and financial payoffs, but little instruction on what to do next. When a huge part of your identity is wrapped up in a company or life passion—often at the expense of everything else—it's easy to then feel some postpartum blues after the exit, even if it made you rich. It is, in part, that desire to once again feel full that leads many of these founders—even after significant payouts leave them set for life—to start another company, and another. When money is no longer a concern, you realize it was never really the primary goal anyway.

In 1998, a group of friends started a company that quickly evolved into a money transfer service. As the company grew, they hired more friends (and people they believed could become great friends) to join their team. It was a tight-knit crew; some even called it a "mafia."[10] In 2002, the company, PayPal, went public, and eBay acquired it for $1.5 billion (an unusually huge sum at the time). Many of those founders and early employees—all of whom became multimillionaires—went on to start some of the largest and most significant companies of our time: Tesla, YouTube, Yelp, LinkedIn—the list goes on. So why, when no one needed the money anymore, would they repeat that grueling process over and over again?

For many people, work offers not only financial security but a sense of community and daily challenge. Others find that sense of purpose in raising a family or in a cherished hobby. But whatever it is, if it suddenly disappears, it's traumatic.

Many of the clients I work with in my practice—both individuals and companies—are in a state of transition. These individuals may have experienced a recent weight loss, a career shift, a geographic move, or a breakup. With companies, those transitions may look a little different: a new merger or acquisition, an organizational restructuring, a leadership change. But a person going through a divorce and a company with slumping sales are more similar than you might think. They are both in mourning and adjusting to the end of one chapter—a great love, a formerly thriving business—while optimistically seeking new opportunities and settling into their new, as-yet-undefined role.

It's no coincidence that so many of my clients are in transition. Those going through changes are already in a state of flux and are looking for help moving in new directions. A career shift or geographic move may lead you to explore a new look, which attracts new social companions and activities, and as a result, the entire rhythm of your life is suddenly transformed. Whatever the circumstances, your receptivity to change—and how you process it—will determine the outcome.

When our favorite television programs end, we often feel a profound sense of loss. The people we've lived with for years, who have entertained us and made us weep, the people we feel really "got us" or that we admired or simply loved to watch behave badly—they grow to feel like family. And when the plug is pulled, it's jarring. Especially if we don't get the closure we want from the finale. Just think of the polarizing finales of some of the most beloved programs: *Mad Men, Seinfeld, Breaking Bad*. So many expectations, so much speculation, so many mixed reviews.

In television, as in life, I find there are three main types of endings: (1) the *Sopranos* and *Lost* style of ending that leaves you wanting, wondering, riddled with questions, and agitated by a sense of incompleteness; (2) the *M*A*S*H* and *Friday Night Lights* ending, which wrap up storylines and character threads into a neat and tidy package, brimming with sentimental satisfaction and even—in the case of *Friday Night Lights*—giving us a glimpse into the future; and (3) perhaps the most enraging and controversial of all, the *Newhart, St. Elsewhere,* and *Roseanne* genre of ending, which throws in a surprise twist and drops a bomb on the loyal, unsuspecting viewer: "Surprise! Nothing you watched was real—the entire run of the show was but a dream! A farce! And the joke's on you."

Ideally, we want our various life finales to fall in the second category. (Incidentally, the much-loved *M*A*S*H* finale is still the single most-watched non-sports television program in history. It's tough to compete with the Super Bowl.[11]) We don't just want answers; we need them. Now. We desire what social psychologist Arie Kruglanski termed "cognitive closure": a firm answer, without ambiguity.[12] Kruglanski's research reveals how the strength of our desire for closure can color everything else—our decisions, biases, impressions, and judgments—to such an extent that it induces a sort of cognitive "freezing."

Each of us ranks differently on this need-for-closure scale, but naturally, the higher the stakes, the more we care. Anything involving money and matters of the heart tends to require specific closure, while less intensely emotional endings can pass by with a shrug. We also tend to vary within different sectors of our own lives. I rank very high on the need-for-closure scale in my personal life. I marvel at people who are seemingly able to move forward without fully understanding how or why a relationship ended. Cliffhangers leave me agitated, and my anxiety spikes. And yet, in my professional life, I'm much more comfortable diving into the unknown.

Like it or not, we are surrounded by change. It envelops us, constantly reminding us that resistance is futile. And while we can't stop it, we can redefine our relationship to it.

Author and organizational consultant William Bridges emphasizes the distinction between change and transition.[13] Change, he argues, happens to us. It disrupts us. Transition, by contrast, is the process of how we deal with that change. He sees change as a type of barrier—something we long to "get past"—whereas transition is a path that begins with the act of letting go.[14]

Bridges outlines three stages of transition:

1. Endings
2. The neutral zone
3. The new beginning

The first stage, *endings*, is emotional. We resist. It may be fraught with fear, anger, and denial. We are stung by a sense of loss. We long to go back to the comfort and familiarity of before. We resist the unknown, even if it's positive and beneficial.

Stage two, *the neutral zone*, disorients us. It's chaotic. Empty. It's the seismic shift from old to new. From then to now. Anxiety mounts. But it's also a time of fertile possibilities. Of maybe and whatif?

In stage three, *the new beginning*, change finally settles in. We find our groove. We become anchored in purpose once more. Excitement replaces anxiety.

2015 was a year of great personal change for me. I began the New Year feeling blessed by life's riches, anchored in optimism, and grateful for stability. I was resettling back into New York for a long-term relationship with the intent to marry and exuding physical vitality. Life was good. Then, within a matter of months, I broke off the relationship, moved back to California, and learned I had a serious health condition that demanded immediate attention. My world turned upside down. Change bombarded me from every angle. The future—the one I thought I could safely predict only a few months prior—now seemed devastatingly uncertain.

The end of my relationship—like the end of any serious relationship—was bittersweet. During the ending phase, nostalgia creeps in, and it becomes difficult to distinguish between a genuine longing for the person and simply a pull toward what you once had. After all, once we officially resign ourselves to the end, we are left in the neutral zone, shivering with emptiness.

And anyone who's ever experienced a personal health scare or that of a loved one understands the weight of medical uncertainty. Our need for closure is at an all-time high. We just want to know, whatever the diagnosis may be, so we can move forward. But even science—perhaps *especially* science—does not have all the answers. Certainly not right away. So we move reluctantly through the first two phases of transition while clinging to the wall of change.

A few more months elapsed, and I finally reached the new beginning phase. New romantic interests popped up (as they inevitably do), and I began to date again, feeling more certain of what I wanted this time and grateful for the hard lessons learned from my recent near-miss. And after a long string of confusing, emotionally charged doctors' visits, invasive procedures, and more-complicated-than-anticipated surgery, the immediate threats to my health dissipated, and I settled into my new life of perpetual monitoring—a constant reminder of both the fragility and resilience of the human body.

We can never predict how these moments of trauma will affect us. We may like to think we know ourselves well enough to feel confident in how we might react when radical change is thrust upon us, but in reality, we can never really anticipate the mental state it will induce and our knee-jerk reactions.

During this time of unanticipated change, I assumed panic would overtake me. That I'd be paralyzed by anxiety, unable to deal with day-to-day reality. But much to my surprise, it didn't. Instead, something entirely different emerged: A feeling of calm. My less-than-ideal circumstances were a complex riddle for me to solve, with each new day revealing a different plot twist. It demanded I be fully present in the moment and filled me with a sense of purpose. Sure, there were extreme lows and emotional distress, and in a larger sense I was still terrified. But it took this forced exit from my old life—from the complacency into which I'd settled—to usher in a new state of existence: I was now living a life in permanent transition, and it wouldn't end when the pangs of heartbreak were replaced by the flutter of newfound love, nor would it evaporate with a clean bill of health.

Sometimes we're ejected from our cozy perch by unforeseen circumstances, thrown out on the street without warning, and it isn't until we arrive there—weary and confused, humbled and hurting—that we submit to a life of blissful uncertainty. It is only when we embrace the fallibility of our relationships, the borrowed time on which we operate, and fully accept that change is always a mere phone call away that we can begin to flourish in transition, in a life lived in-between. Because change is not coming—it's here. And leveling up is not achieved through a billion-dollar exit. It is secured moment by moment, through disappointments and triumphs alike. Our grandest exits are often the ones we never intended to make.

SCRUM MASTER CHEAT SHEET

In the words of Doc Brown, "Where we're going, we don't need roads."[15] But even a winged-door DeLorean won't make the journey into the unknown less frightening. So how can we remain receptive to change, ready to transition in small and large ways alike? Here are three strategies for making an exit that blasts you into the future without forsaking the past.

☛ TRAIN YOUR BRAIN FOR CHANGE. Gretchen Rubin's latest book, *Better Than Before*, teaches us how to harness the power of habit formation.[16] Habits—the good ones—are the key to change, and therefore a crucial link to happiness. When we channel our self-control into positive habits, we commit to the cultivation of a better life and reap the rewards. But there's also a downside to a habitualized life. Anchoring our behavior too rigidly in habits can render us inflexible and consequently less receptive to the benefits of the unknown and unanticipated.

But don't stop flossing yet. You can maintain good habits while still allowing for some flexibility. You can create an anti-habit habit through ABC: Always. Be. Changing. When change becomes your default, it's less jarring to your system. And when you inevitably get hit with a curveball that forces you into large-scale change, your freak-out factor is greatly diminished. We are so often told the virtue of routine and efficiency that we often forget the rewards of novelty and conscious disruption. So invert the habit trend and regularly introduce small changes into your schedule. Take the scenic route, try a new fitness challenge, cook one new recipe a week—anything that makes you adjust to the unfamiliar on a regular basis. When your brain is in the ABC mindset, surprise is a daily occurrence, diminishing the cause for alarm. Stay in charge by mentally embracing change before it thrusts itself upon you.

☞ **SURF FEAR.** Sun-bleached beach bums and ocean-side bonfires. Surfing is often associated with Zenned-out dudes with laid-back attitudes, but it's also an intense, extreme sport. From getting caught in a riptide to becoming shark bait, the dangers of surfing plague even the most seasoned professionals. But riding waves—particularly big ones—floods the body with adrenaline and the happy chemical dopamine, which is a pretty gnarly experience that keeps many surfers chasing waves for life. So how do these salty fanatics overcome the fear factor and hang loose?

Fear is the nemesis of transitioning, able to stop you in your tracks. But you can't remain stagnant on a wave. It's always in motion, and the only option is to move forward. So whatever you fear, find a way to surf it. Whether it's taking an improv class or asking someone out, you can replicate the surfer's high by taking the plunge wherever fear swirls and taunts you. Because even if it doesn't go as planned (hint: it probably won't), the simple act of moving forward will be exhilarating. Putting yourself out there is rewarding, even without some exterior metric of success. Get barreled by fear. It may get sloppy and close out on you, but there's always another wave. And sometimes just paddling out is enough.

☞ **RITUALIZE CLOSURE.** "We must be willing to get rid of the life we've planned, so as to have the life that is waiting for us."[17] For mythologist Joseph Campbell, rituals link us to something larger than ourselves. They allow us to go beyond our physicality and transcend time, as our particular lives link with that which is universal and timeless.[18] They create both intimacy and distance, which allows us to put life in perspective, while also ceremonially bridging us from one reality to the next—from past to present to the still undiscovered. They're life checkpoints, mindfully marking time and bringing us closer to what we might become.

Our life finales are rarely (er, never) packaged in carefully scripted one-hour segments. So when we're handed an emotional cliffhanger, we're left to rely on our own ingenuity to create the closure we need. Ritualizing how we deal with endings can induce feelings of comfort in the wake of uncertainty. From internal expressions of gratitude and forgiveness to the simple acknowledgement of what nourished and what depleted us, ritualized reflections are cleansing pauses that soothe the emotional upheaval of change. Formally recognizing the passing of an era can yield more peace of mind than weeks of sleepless questioning and analysis. It's a ritual of detachment meant not to deny the past, but to welcome the future.

THE LAZY LOWDOWN: TOP TEN CHAPTER TAKEAWAYS

1. Betting on bigger isn't always better. Know when enough is enough.
2. Finales disappoint. Create your own closure.
3. We can't know what's next until we find distance from the past.
4. Transitions are a process, not an overnight acquisition.
5. When what we thought defined us ceases to exist, life's unanticipated riches may start to pay out.
6. Embrace a life in transition. Eject yourself from complacency.
7. Change is not coming. It's already here.
8. Forced exits can be the best exits.
9. Hang ten on fear's frothy swell—and enjoy the ride.
10. Always. Be. Changing.

12.

Hitting Refresh

THE LIFE PIVOT

Tell me, what is it you plan to do with your one wild and precious life?

—MARY OLIVER, *The Summer Day*

Evan was already a seasoned entrepreneur when he quit his job at Google to start a podcasting company in 2004. But just as his company was ready to launch, Apple released iTunes—complete with an iPod podcasting platform.[1] He was screwed.

His company, Odeo, needed a new direction. Not just a feature that would differentiate it from Apple, but a completely new offering. So they hosted some hackathons, where developers and product people came together to "hack" together new solutions.[2] One of Odeo's employees, Jack, rose to the top of the brainstorming pool. He had a vision for a technical tool that highlighted what a person was doing at any given moment—their "status." It was SMS meets blogging meets social networking, but while it drew on all these existing platforms, it wasn't quite like any of them. And it definitely wasn't a podcasting company.

Evan put Jack in charge of the project, and on March 21, 2006, Jack sent out the first message: "Just setting up my twttr."[3] Jack Dorsey's idea, which was launched as a side project within Evan Williams's would-be podcasting company, later became Twitter. It was the company's do-over—not its original plan—that rose to become one of our dominant communication tools.

Startups often "pivot"—or change course—when their initial venture doesn't turn out as planned. Sometimes the pivot is just a twist in their approach, while other times it means scratching the initial idea and starting over completely. Pivoting isn't bad or embarrassing; sometimes it's just necessary. It allows you to pull from all your accumulated knowledge and redirect yourself toward something better. It's not just a step away from something—it's a step toward something else.

Some pivots happen early on, before the company has much traction or exposure. The story goes that YouTube, the world's most popular video platform, started as a dating site called Tune In Hook Up, inspired by the site Hot or Not.[4] Needless to say, it took a sharp turn early on (and probably for the best). Or take Soylent, a startup that makes meal replacement beverages. Three former participants in the accelerator Y-Combinator were running out of money, and their initial project (inexpensive cell phone towers) had failed. So while they scrambled to make ends meet, one of the founders noticed that eating—something they annoyingly had to do multiple times a day—was a huge time suck. So they abandoned software development and launched stomach-first into a quest to replace the need to eat. As of 2015, they'd raised over $22 million in funding—proving many people share their desire to forgo food.[5] Sometimes you're just a pivot away from a major breakthrough—professionally or personally.

One summer a few years ago I was unhappy. Really unhappy. I was tired of where and how I lived. I was teaching—which I loved—but the time commitment didn't allow me to travel spontaneously or pursue other long-term projects, and it held me back from other, more lucrative ventures. I was still living in New York, a city I once revered, but my gripes were beginning to outweigh my adoration and several close friends had already left. I was also single, without any promising prospects on the horizon. I felt stuck. I felt stagnant. But I wasn't sure how to fix it.

So, still unsure of what I wanted to move toward, I committed to a life pivot and imposed a six-month deadline on myself to make a move. Any move. I placed no limits or parameters, casting the net wide as I searched for my "next big thing"—or just a temporary stop-over on my journey. Whichever came first. This unconditional openness almost led me to work with the military in combat zones in Afghanistan (my mother is grateful that plan did not pan out). But while I ultimately didn't relocate to the Middle East, just the process of considering it reinvigorated me with a new sense of purpose. I felt alive, excited, driven, and terrified. When that plan fell through, I wanted more of that feeling, one I hadn't felt in a while. Life suddenly looked different even without any substantive changes. My mind was already pivoting.

My imaginings repeatedly drifted west to California—a place I often visited, always wishing I lived there. I had several reasons for initially traveling west: a different pace of life, a change of scenery, nice weather, and easy access to the ocean—at least these were the reasons I cited when pressed. But I also had another reason that I was more reluctant to articulate. California would allow me to break free from my New York identity and explore an alternative, softer persona. My fiery personality and professional drive didn't disappear when I stepped out of New York, but they did manifest themselves differently: West Coast me goes to the farmer's market; she takes quiet walks along the water; her friendships—while fewer—are deeper and more consistent; she plays outside every day and hikes in nature; she goes to bed earlier and wakes up earlier; and she spends nights on the couch without feeling guilty or thinking she's missing something. Both my New York and California selves enjoy simple pleasures, domesticity, and entertaining, but these affinities are nurtured far more in the Golden State than the Empire State.

So, what I mean to say is: I had a hunch. A hunch that when West Coast me could flourish I would finally be the kind of person I wanted to be, not just in my private life but in general. I knew California was where I wanted to be not because it seemed professionally advantageous at the time—the barometer for most of my other important life decisions up to that point—but because that was where my heart was. That was where I felt like the best version of myself. I could name endless reasons why it was irrational and irresponsible to stop teaching, leave my established community, and give up my rent-stabilized apartment—after all, those are what had kept me from taking the plunge earlier. But once I created a pivot imperative, imposed a deadline, and removed my usual barriers, the floodgates of opportunity opened.

It's no coincidence that, shortly thereafter, not one but several professional opportunities presented themselves in California, including a potential talent acquisition of my startup. I acted without hesitation: after 16 years in New York, I up and moved to California in only two weeks. I gave notice to everyone and quit the life I'd known for so long. Not because I'd thought through every conceivable way in which it might go wrong but because there was so much that might go right.

My hunch did not lead me astray: While I moved west to follow my heart, to change the pace and quality of my life, my career kicked into overdrive almost immediately upon my arrival. The initial project that brought me out there eventually changed course, but I seamlessly found myself with more possibilities than ever before—from running incubators to leading international innovation workshops with Fortune 500 companies. A personally motivated pivot ushered in a time of professional flourishing. My career spiked when I stopped trying to fit into a prescribed mold of what people thought I should be doing (working in fashion, teaching); of what I told myself I should be doing (raising oodles of VC money if I ever wanted my startups to succeed); and of where the masses concluded I needed to be to "make it" (New York—and only New York). Instead, I inverted all of those assumptions: What if I focused on building a company that didn't require venture capital? And what if I did it on a completely different coast, among a community of relative strangers? Instead of moving forward with a carefully structured strategic plan, culling from input from everyone around me, I took a leap that was part impulse, part long-time longing.

A fresh start. A clean slate. How many times have you daydreamed of starting over? If not with your whole life, then some specific aspect of it?

Flipping the mental switch that permits you to hit "refresh" with wild abandon isn't easy. It's not accessed through a detailed strategic plan, an exhaustive analysis of every possible outcome, or a list of how to mitigate risk at every turn. Rather, it looks like something you've likely forgotten about—something you may have lost touch with long ago: play.

To be clear, play is not something you do during your normal, everyday time. It's separate. It's a sort of time-out-of-time experience that's not part of your usual productivity routine. It begins and it ends. It's limited—but those limitations seep into and reverberate through the other corners of your life, long after playtime has officially wound down. The historian Johan Huizinga refers to us as *Homo Ludens,* or "Man the Player."[6] Play, he argues, predates culture and is the foundation for everything from romantic attachment to religious ritual. And it is this connection to spiritual rituals that further emphasizes the sacred nature of play—something to be protected and revered, not casually dismissed or relegated exclusively to the realm of children. Play is serious business.

Al and Tipper Gore, in their book *Joined at the Heart,* argue that "play is a kind of aerobic workout for the human capacity to change."[7] Like most worthwhile things, reaping the rewards of play takes conditioning and practice. But it is through play that we not only prepare for change but embody it. It's how we imagine alternative possibilities for ourselves in ways both big and small. Play permits us to step outside the confines of our current existence and explore the world beyond.

But despite the fact that nearly everyone enjoys play, we bury it at the end of our life's to-do list. "Who has time for play?" you might ask. But when re-examined as a sacred rite that conditions us for renewal, you may instead ask, "Can I afford *not* to play?" Philosopher Ludwig Wittgenstein wrote, "If people did not sometimes do silly things, nothing intelligent would ever get done."[8] However counterintuitive it may seem, play makes good sense.

Many of the things we discipline ourselves to prioritize have direct benefits. But play is not like a test you can study for or a new health regimen that offers quantitative results. It's more elusive. So how do we find our play outlets—and how do we know if they are working?

The Central Park Dance Skaters Association (CPDSA) is a nonprofit organization that offers free roller skating and live DJ music in New York's Central Park from April through October.

The group first began meeting on Central Park's Dead Road just down from the band shelter, in the late seventies, only to be pushed out for lack of a formal permit by the mid-nineties. But the skaters refused to roll away quietly and organized to obtain all the necessary documentation to keep the skate circle alive. They now legally barricade off the area and amplify their music every weekend afternoon. But don't let the barricades fool you—the beauty of the skate circle is its inclusivity. Can't skate? No problem. They'd love to have you come in and dance with them (one elderly regular just stands in the center and bounces feverishly to the music).

As you might imagine, colorful characters abound: There's Bladie Flowness, in his neon, handmade costumes that bear his name and image, rolling in on his half-electric, dragon-headed bicycle and selling his latest mix CDs. Then there's the chiseled shirtless guy (I've never once seen him put on a shirt, no matter how low the temperature drops) who balances water bottles on his head while he skates. Or the other chiseled shirtless guy (who only skates backward while flexing his pecs). Or the Hollywood Roller Twins who are neither connected to Hollywood nor twins, but they do dress alike and skate in unison—and for what it's worth, I've known them for years and still can't tell them apart. Or there's Leslie, the much-beloved, recently deceased, ponytailed octogenarian leader who only wore purple. (When I went to his apartment to have him fit me for some custom skates, I learned he not only wore all purple, but he lived completely in purple, right down to bottles of purple Vitamin Water and cushy purple cat beds. That is, with the exception of the kitchen: It was red.)

CPDSA is an adult playpen, and for me and many others, it's one of the happiest places on Earth. In fact, I would argue it's actually impossible for everything *not* to be great once you step into the skate circle. I've been down, exhausted, and/or hungover prior to many skate sessions, but the minute I arrive, I'm greeted by such an overwhelming surge of warmth and positive energy that the rest of the world melts away. Couple that sense of community with the driving beat of soulful music and the physical flow state achieved by a few spins on your retro quads, layered with the enthusiastic cheers from eager onlookers, and it's hard to characterize the skate circle as anything less than magical.

Magic. It's something in which we all once believed. When we were kids, an old rug became a flying carpet, and a plastic sword was infused with superpowers. These are the "enchanted objects" of our youth.[9] And it's no surprise that superhero movies top the box office charts, or that the cult of *Star Wars* wages indefatigably on, attracting audiences of all ages. Outside the theater, magic is hard to locate and even harder to maintain in our adult lives.

Inside spaces like the skate circle, names, jobs, and financial statuses are irrelevant. I can't tell you the last name or occupation of most of the people I've hugged and swapped sweat with for the better part of a decade, and I don't really care to learn them. I never ask, and they don't offer; somehow delving too deeply into life's stark realities seems offensive in the sacred space of the circle. It squashes the magic.

But is there an age where the magic inevitably wanes? Where even roller skates can't wheel in the ability to pivot and play?

A study of over 500 founders of successful companies in high-growth industries revealed that the majority of first-time founders were not in their twenties (as the tech world might have us believe). Rather, the average age when they launched their first venture was 40 years old, and the majority were married with kids.[10] We often hear of the 22-year-old wunderkinds who abandon school and make their first millions pre-25. But for every Mark Zuckerberg, there's a comparable "late bloomer" who finds their footing and reinvents themselves a bit later in life.

Chaja Rubinstein was born in Poland in 1870 (or 1871 or possibly '72, depending on the source). She traded in her given name for her preferred name, Helena Juliet Rubinstein, when she moved to Australia at 24. At 33, she began selling her Valaze face cream in Melbourne, but she didn't enter the U.S. market until the age of 45. (This was still a time when women could not obtain bank loans, so Rubinstein paid in cash for everything.) In 1928, at the age of 58, she sold her eponymous cosmetics company to Lehman Brothers for $7.3 million. The company tanked under the new leadership, and when the Depression hit and the stock market crashed shortly thereafter, she bought the company back for $1 million, only to go on to restore its profitability and scale the company even further. Over the years, Rubinstein partied with the likes of Marcel Proust and enlisted Joan Miró and Salvador Dalí as her designers. At 68, she divorced her first husband and married a Georgian prince 23 years her junior. Rather than "Helena" or Ms. Rubinstein, she preferred to simply be called "Madame."[11] In short, Madame was a supreme badass.

Helena Rubinstein transformed our relationship with cosmetics. She was famous for her declaration, "There are no ugly women. Only lazy ones." Needless to say, she did not mince words. She was eccentric, blunt, and lived large—at 4'10", she was not big in stature, yet her personality and drive filled every room she entered. Helena remained at the helm of her company until her death at 92 (or 94, as the case may be).[12]

Helena Rubinstein is one of my entrepreneurial heroes. She was a self-made success, a pioneer in her field, and one of the shrewdest and wealthiest women in the world at her time (and yet she's sadly unknown to most people). From her initial move to Australia to the repurchase of her company, she reinvented herself and staged a comeback again and again, well into an age when many would have written her off.

Rubinstein's archrival was Elizabeth Arden, another impressive businesswoman and early cosmetics mogul. Both women were savvy entrepreneurs who knew what they wanted—and how to get it—in both their professional and personal lives. They died within only 18 months of each other—Rubinstein in 1965 and Arden in 1966—but sadly never spoke directly to one another (by all accounts).[13] Rubinstein and Arden also paved the way for Estée Lauder, another beauty industry titan who didn't formally establish her company until she was nearly 40 (and who also changed her name to suit the persona she wished to project).[14] Whether you're a college dropout or a corporate executive looking for a second act, it's never too early or too late for a life pivot.

So how do you find your play outlets—and how do you know if they're moving you in the right direction?

I'm what you might call a karaoke enthusiast, but that hasn't always been the case. Years ago, I'd tag along with a few friends who were seasoned regulars at a midtown dive in NYC. They'd expertly croon their standard set of duets, and I'd marvel at their gumption to sing publicly. Then one day I stepped out of the shadows and gave it a shot. Trembling, I queued up the song from the first 45 record I ever owned: "Elvira" by the Oak Ridge Boys. Much to my surprise, I wasn't half bad. So I moved onto Linda Ronstadt, Dusty Springfield, and Gladys Knight. I'd officially caught the fever. In the years that followed, I hosted monthly karaoke parties—some were wild and costumed, like the Valentine's Day pants-optional parties and the annual "santaoke" holiday event, while others brought together shy tech nerds who also liked to break loose in song. The parties took place in everything from tiki bars to basements dives, ranging in size from seven people to well over a hundred, frequented by artists, academics, and bankers alike. It was a late night melting pot, a sort of musical mosh pit, equal parts singing fest and down-and-dirty dance party, where you never knew what might happen next. Each month, eight hours and hundreds of songs flew by in a flash, accompanied by the shimmering beat of the tambourine and a roaming cowbell, punctuated with spontaneous shouts and claps. I never made a cent on the parties, and I don't have much to show for them other than embarrassing photos. But they were some of the best nights of my life.

I didn't seek out karaoke any more than I did the skate circle. These weren't lifelong goals, and they certainly weren't directly contributing to my professional advancement. I never penciled them into my life plan. But once I found them, I couldn't imagine my life without them. I threw myself into these playtime rituals with the same fervor I did the rest of my life. My world changed dramatically when I moved to California, but it also shifted in more subtle ways when I made time for these less obvious yet equally essential pursuits.

Rumi, the great mystic, asks, "Why do you seek water when you are the stream?"[15] He believes we are the source of our own fulfillment—if we allow ourselves to access it. For that which we seek, also seeks us:

> *No lover seeks union without the beloved also seeking . . .*
> *No sound of clapping comes from only one hand.*
> *The thirsty man is moaning, "O delicious water!"*
> *The water is calling, "Where is the one who will drink me?"*
> *The thirst in all our souls is the magnetism of the Water . . .*[16]

But what is it you seek? And are you allowing it to find you?

C. S. Lewis dedicates his book *The Lion, the Witch and the Wardrobe* to his goddaughter, Lucy Barfield: "I wrote this story for you, but when I began it I had not realized that girls grow quicker than books. As a result you are already too old for fairy tales, and by the time it is printed and bound you will be older still. Some day you will be old enough to start reading fairy tales again."[17] When can we give ourselves permission to fantasize and dream once more? At what age? After which achievement? The pivots that matter most start and end in your mind. They diverge sharply from your scripted plan and probably seem a little out-there at first—they wear a lot of purple and sing way too loudly. But that's right when the story gets interesting. The fantasies start to become a reality at the intersection of your practical accomplishments and your daydreams. The next chapter awaits you. And you're both author and star.

SCRUM MASTER CHEAT SHEET

Living life as a startup isn't about a single accomplishment. Instead, we're invited to pivot repeatedly and become the serial reinventors of our own lives—not just at the major milestones and forced exit points but perpetually along the way. Here's how to stay fresh and hit refresh on the regular.

☛ **KEEP IT SPICY: DIVERSIFY.** At the beginning of the twentieth century, Michio Suzuki had a flourishing looms business that boomed for over thirty years. And yet, despite that prosperity, Suzuki decided to diversify—to branch out beyond weaving. So, after some market research, he decided to add cars to his portfolio, and within two years, he produced a prototype. World War II halted the car production, but textile manufacturing was thriving—until the tide turned again and eventually the cotton market declined. Suzuki returned to motor vehicles once more, this time shifting his focus to a different variety of transportation: a motorized bike, or motorcycle. Suzuki didn't wait until his current industry bottomed out to start dabbling in other prospects. He understood that change was imminent and proactively sought opportunities before desperation necessitated it.

When it comes to your financial portfolio, the theory behind diversification is that it diminishes risk. Put in more colloquial terms, we're encouraged not to put all our eggs in one basket. But the real motivation for diversification in your everyday life is not just about mitigating risk; diversification also multiplies your potential bounty. Diversifying your life—financially, professionally, socially—doesn't make you a dilettante. It creates a wealth of options, both now and in the future, and at the very least, it informs your current course in unimaginable ways. Entrepreneurs profess repeatedly that while it's easy to wear blinders and only focus on what seems like the critical and important stuff, it's the pursuit of ideas and activities outside the scope of those interests that often delivers a fresh perspective or leads to an unlikely solution. Focus is important, but focus without the inspired novelty of diversity limits and grows stale. Plus, some like it hot. And variety keeps life spicy.

☞ PRIORITIZE PLAY. Like many people, I had a rich imagination as a child. Any given day bustled with make-believe scenarios, like playing house under my carefully constructed blanket forts, or running a store with my old typewriter and empty grocery containers, or teaching imaginary school with my mini desk and easel. I organized neighborhood talent shows where other able-bodied youth and I lip-synced choreographed performances to The Supremes on the front lawn of our apartment complex, a free show for any neighbor willing to merely step outside their door. I regularly created improvised skits with friends (far too few of which were video recorded), circulating endlessly through absurd realities, far-fetched characters, and, of course, costumes.

No childhood is complete without playing dress-up. I kept a dedicated costume bin full of my mother's discarded clothing and other miscellaneous treasures from early childhood well into adulthood. The bin and its contents shifted slightly over the years, but much of it remained consistent, throwbacks to bygone styles and eras. (For the record, I eventually downsized for space-saving reasons, not because I outgrew dress-up.) The world of pretend that spiraled out of those sartorial seeds, however, perpetually refreshed itself.

Polish writer Sławomir Mrożek compares the world we inhabit to "a market-stall filled with fancy dresses and surrounded by crowds seeking their 'selves'. One can change dresses without end, so what a wondrous liberty the seekers enjoy. Let's go on searching for our real selves, it's smashing fun—on condition that the real self will never be found. Because if it were, the fun would end."[18] The popularity of events like Burning Man, in which tribes of grown-ups annually abscond to Nevada's Black Rock desert for a week of off-the-grid costumed revelry, indicate that the merits and allure of playing dress-up has firmly embedded itself in the modern adult psyche. We may not regularly pull out the costume box during our adult playtime, but regardless of our ongoing relationship with an actual costume bin, playing pretend is a fertile metaphor for the transformative power of play.

Play often occurs during ritualized, set times during childhood, and that regimented approach equally benefits adults. So schedule regular play time—either alone or with a play date—because if you don't schedule it, it's likely other demands on your time will inevitably take precedent. As author Tom Robbins argues, "It's never too late to have a happy childhood."[19] So make time for magic. Regular play strengthens bonds and encourages self-discovery, which lays the foundation for both current and future pivots. (Oh, and as a bonus: it's fun.)

☞ **SEIZE "GOOD ENOUGH."** We are warned time and again—by over-achievers, not slouches, for the record—about the downfalls of a life lived in pursuit of perfection. From "perfect is the enemy of good" (an oft-cited phrase attributed to Voltaire, who arrived at it via an Italian proverb)[20]; to General George S. Patton's alleged pronouncement that "a good plan violently executed today is far and away better than a perfect plan next week"; to Alexander Watson-Watt, the inventor of the English radar, who championed "the cult of the imperfect" with the directive to "give them the third best to go on with; the second best comes too late, the best never comes."[21] In other words, the answer to "when?" is *now*. Whether you're looking to run a marathon, start a relationship, or launch a business, whatever big adventure you want to embark on can start right now. Sure, there are some variables that can and should sway the nuances of your decision, but waiting for "someday" shouldn't be one of them. The timing will never be perfect. *You* will never be perfect. And the outcome, no matter how long you wait, will always be less than perfect. But nothing great was founded on perfection. So get ready to make your move in all its imperfect glory.

THE LAZY LOWDOWN: TOP TEN CHAPTER TAKEAWAYS

1. Pivot your life toward happiness.
2. Vow to clean the slate. Take a leap that's part impulse, part longing, and a lot of fun.

3. Flip the mental switch that auto-refreshes the browser of your life.
4. Get serious: start playing.
5. It's never too early or too late to find your footing and reinvent yourself.
6. Diversify now, not when you're down and desperate.
7. Dig deep into the costume bin, hop on your flying carpet, and reclaim the magic.
8. Find your skate circle: the happiest place on earth.
9. Champion good enough so you have a chance at really great.
10. Don't forget once-upon-a-time fairy tales. But don't just start reading them again. Rewrite them.

Conclusion:
Free Falling in the Arena

THE
ENTREPRENEURIAL
EXPEDITION
OF YOUR LIFE

We don't have to become heroes overnight.

—ELEANOR ROOSEVELT, *You Learn By Living*

Teddy Roosevelt became the youngest president in history after the assassination of President McKinley. While attempting to win a third term, he failed to secure his party's nomination, so he founded an entirely new party—the Progressive Bull Moose Party—and ran on its ticket. After an upsetting defeat, he set out to absolve himself of that disappointment by embarking on an expedition through the Amazon down the River of Doubt (later renamed the Roosevelt River). Throughout the treacherous journey into a remote and previously unexplored region, Teddy and his crew battled disease, hunger, insects, environmental hazards, and human attacks. Several men died along the way, and Teddy only narrowly cheated death from extreme fever and a leg injury.[1]

Teddy was an energetic, physical force of nature. "When he came into the room, it was as if a strong wind had blown the door open," wrote conservationist John Burroughs.[2] He revered what he called "the strenuous life": success through strenuous effort and triumph over hardship.[3] He embodied this in his own life, which—while remarkable in many ways—was simultaneously riddled with tragedies and failures. And whenever they surfaced, he attacked these setbacks vigorously, both physically and mentally, constantly testing his own limits.

In a speech at the Sorbonne in 1910, Teddy Roosevelt delivered what became one of his most famous rhetorical passages:

> It is not the critic who counts; not the man who points out how the strong man stumbles or where the doer of deeds could have done them better. The credit belongs to the man who is actually in the arena, whose face is marred by dust and sweat and blood; who strives valiantly; who errs, who comes short again and again, because there is no effort without error and shortcoming; but who does actually strive to do the deeds; who knows great enthusiasms, the great devotions; who spends himself in a worthy cause; who at the best knows in the end the triumph of high achievement, and who at the worst, if he fails, at least fails while daring greatly, so that his place shall never be with those cold and timid souls who neither know victory nor defeat.[4]

For Teddy, being in the action—not standing idly on the fringes—is what counts. Trying and failing is triumphant—passivity is not. Surviving danger, hardship, and toil produces greatness. He advocates "not for the life of ease but for the life of strenuous endeavor."[5] We travel down the River of Doubt repeatedly in life, and those expeditions have the power to shape us the most. But we must remain in the arena to experience them.

Politicians don't often spring to mind when we think of our twenty-first-century innovators. But there is one family of leaders that exemplifies the power of living life as a startup: the Roosevelts. Theodore, Franklin, and Eleanor embodied many of the qualities discussed throughout this book. From the New Deal to the National Parks, the Roosevelts may not have launched companies, but they did collectively innovate with an entrepreneurial spirit for over a hundred years. (Ken Burns has even dedicated 14 hours of film to their fascinating lives.[6]) What's most compelling about the Roosevelts is the fact that, regardless of how we individually view their respective political actions, it is hard to contest that they were, quite simply, extraordinary human beings. Not just for their grand political accomplishments but for the intentional and steadfast ways they lived their lives. They were flawed, yet fearless. And that's really the most we can ask of ourselves.

So how will you design your life?

Writer Annie Dillard speaks to the distinction between individual days lived and the collective accumulation of those days that comprise a life: "How we spend our days is, of course, how we spend our lives. There is no shortage of good days. It is good lives that are hard to come by."[7] Are we striving for good days or good lives? And are they at odds? Happiness isn't determined by the daily peaks and valleys—it unfolds over a lifetime. And while being present and living for the moment fosters well-being, life—and happiness—is best played as a long game. We don't always have a clear view of the forest at every point in the journey, so a single tree's branches shouldn't trip us up.

LinkedIn founder Reid Hoffman describes starting a company as "throwing yourself off a cliff and assembling an airplane on the way down."[8] So, too, are many of the most challenging and gratifying aspects of life—we're free falling, piecing it all together on the way down, hoping for the best. But do we have the courage to jump off that cliff in the first place?

Eleanor Roosevelt puts the merits of courage into perspective: "Courage is more exhilarating than fear and in the long run it is easier. We do not have to become heroes overnight. Just a step at a time, meeting each new thing that comes up, seeing it is not as dreadful as it appeared, discovering we have the strength to stare it down."[9] In the courage vs. fear stare down, courage understands the long-view strategy while fear gets caught in the brush. But for courage to dominate, we must give ourselves permission to grow over time, incrementally, day by day. A life lived in the arena is heroic, even if it's not always remarkable.

Silicon Valley is rooted in the creation of disruptive technology. It churns out innovative concepts and products, scales them, and leaves older, larger companies questioning where they went wrong as they play catch-up. Your challenge is not to invent a new viral app or be the next Elon Musk. It's simply to construct a disruptive identity. This may seem like a daunting task, but the great news about innovation is it isn't spawned from one defining choice, nor is it built completely from scratch. Rather, it stems from what already exists. The best innovators don't recreate the wheel each day. They layer on the past, pulling from experiences and failures alike, and use them to develop something new but familiar. After all, most "failures" are near-misses, not total catastrophes, leaving a lot of raw material to work with—not just useless debris.

Living your life like a startup means strategically taking control of the journey, while also making space for some free-falling improvisation. Joseph Campbell says to "follow your bliss"—but as we now know, that's only one piece of the happiness puzzle.[10] Here's a more complete 12-step guide for your expedition:

1. Start by reminding yourself that life as an MVP can never start too early or too late. This outlook puts you in testing mode and eliminates waste, which lightens the load of living—and makes it a lot more interesting. As an MVP, you're lean, flexible, and firing on feedback. The way you solve problems may not look fancy, but the quick-and-dirty approach will give you a competitive advantage. Happiness and practicality are not always complementary, but they need not be contradictory ("practicality" may need some conceptual rejiggering). And since the results of your smoke tests may defy logic and surprise you, don't get caught in your equivalent of the law-school-default trap and give up on your potato-salad-making whims too early. Ask yourself the hard questions that strip away the fatty outer layers and take you deep into your core—force yourself to validate your choices to yourself before others.

2. As you slip into your imperfect MVP state, your mind will likely resist, so start kneading it into action. The first order of mental business is recalibrating your relationship with risk. Catastrophizing is paralyzing, and obsessing over uncertainty leads you down a negativity death spiral. On the other hand, overzealous positivity and optimism bias are equally dangerous—as are unchecked passions. Instead, find balance by interrogating your passions, anchored with equal parts practicality and positivity, and top it off with the secret sauce that too often gets lost in the optimism shuffle: hard work. That mental recipe builds a channel between your head and your heart, keeping a steady flow of communication between the two.

3. Once you've put your mind through innovation basic training, it's time to get down to business. Your life is an experimental petri dish, and you're never too big to tinker. Fortunately, you can leave your lucky rabbit's foot at home, as you'll make your own luck through decisive action and intuitive resilience. Science

trumps luck through the *observe, hypothesize, test, and repeat* process. For this and every season, planning is out and experimenting is in. And whether the experiments yield the outcome you predicted or desired, or take you down another path altogether, simply eliminating what doesn't work is a victory unto itself. It's all part of the panoramic picture, so don't discount the power of the small stuff.

4. If experimentation does its job (and it usually does), it will not only teach you a few things but also help you unlearn as you go along. Mental models frame our world and color our reality, but they also put us on autopilot and leave us trapped in a presumptive ditch. Consciously straying from conventional wisdom frees you from the binds of groupthink and illuminates whatever you're taking for granted. To jump-start the path to unlearning, get lost—physically or mentally, which will push mental boundaries and shift perspectives. That expansion invalidates assumptions, breeds empathy, and minimizes missed connections. But don't be fooled: mental models are stubborn, and unlearning is just as hard as learning. So start today, but don't expect a clean slate overnight.

5. Recalibrating your perspectives happens in direct relation to understanding the world around you. What do they want, expect, and need? We're social animals, and finding your own version of product-market fit allows you to connect more meaningfully with your audience. What matters to you? What matters to them? That's the point where everyone wins. But it's not just *what* you're delivering to the world—it's also *how*. We thrive and excel not just by producing great work but also by touching people along the way. Mindful investments in what you create and how you deliver it to the world raises both your market value and your probability of happiness. Make like Mickey Drexler and be the Merchant Prince of your own life: obsess over details and probe into the hearts and minds of those around you. (You'll be rewarded for your efforts.)

6. You've taken a hard look at the world around you, now turn the magnifying glass around. The way you self-present reflects not only who you are today but the person you hope to become—the way you want to be treated, the conversations you hope to have, the opportunities you seek. You must be seen before you can be heard. Our identities are fluid, so it's natural to try on visual personas, which in no way diminishes your claim to authenticity. Rather, an "authentic" appearance is, in many ways, an extension of your personal product-market fit: it's the intersection of looking like you belong while also expressing individuality—your flavor and flair. We are all impersonators with a closet full of masks, and your ability to perpetually adapt and transform determines the potency of your social capital.

7. Our mediated lives matter as much as our fleshy existence. We now live in public, and as you may have noticed, your digital self likely has it going on, thanks to constant technical touch-ups. While they do require maintenance, these online outlets also provide space to explore and experiment with different personas. Your virtual self is your surrogate—just like you, only better (or, occasionally, worse). Our online identities intertwine with our off-screen existence. And while your digital life might not always seem like reality, it is not without consequence.

8. Being visually effective is about looking "right," not fashionable. And wealth is more of a state of mind than a number. Money *can* make you happy, but only if you spend it strategically. Expand your definition of "necessity" while also becoming a financial MacGyver to maximize happiness dividends. You don't need a windfall of cash or an elite pedigree to manufacture personal happiness. Hustling and bootstrapping are better than "bad money" with unwanted strings attached. Tight resources force you to maximize the abundance of human capital in your life. You're far richer than you think you are.

9. Now that you're thinking of yourself like a startup, it's time to complicate that equation with a plus-one. Partnerships are as risky as they are rewarding. But for most of us, our romantic mental models don't serve us. Kick Love Santa to the curb and go rogue: become a relationship entrepreneur in how you look for love—and how you keep it. Finding lasting relationship flow involves a feeling, a choice, and (like everything else worth having) ongoing investment and effort. We're only as good as the company we keep *and* the effort we put into keeping that company around. Don't fear baggage—make it work for you. And when in doubt, opt for brave and bold. Its flame burns brightest.

10. Try as we may, relationships fail. We fail. A lot. So once you figure out all the ways you can optimize your life, it's time to give yourself permission to fall down. Because success—at anything—rarely happens on the first try. Your next go-round could be your Angry Birds moment. Or it may be a happy accident that leads to something altogether unexpected. So make space for failure and wear it proudly. When the charms of failure eventually wear thin, follow these rules to make every loss a win: Find newfound resilience through active reflection, know your limits, and plot your comeback.

11. The best part of failure is that it primes you for change. But change doesn't come easily. We move toward and through it like running through mud—it's more of a slow foot drag than a sprint. It's ok to crave closure, but you're more likely to find yourself in the midst of a season finale cliffhanger than a Hollywood wrap-up. Settle into a life in transition (spoiler alert: you're going to be there a while) and ride the wave of fear into a new beginning.

12. So there you are. You did it. You made your exit—but now what? Where do you go from there? Defy logic and play your way into revealing your next move. Give yourself the license to imagine, without the usual constraints of everyday life. Don't worry:

You won't stay floating around on your magic carpet forever, but the ride will allow you to figure out where you'd like to land. And the more you embrace imperfection, the more likely you are to settle into your happy place.

Throughout these pages, as we moved more elaborately through this 12-step guide, I offered dozens of tactics for happiness and over a hundred mantras to live by—enough fodder for a lifetime's worth of exits and pivots. And so I leave you not with more strategies to startup your life, but with the foundational tenets that I hope will blanket your journey, give you comfort, and ground you as you take flight:

☞ **THERE IS VALUE IN BEING ALONE.** One of the most striking differences between the way great leaders like the Roosevelts lived and our current state of existence is their ability to carve out moments of solitude and maintain privacy, even in such public positions. The Roosevelts were able to retreat into the wilderness and spend isolated, deliberate time alone or with family and friends, away from the eyes of the press or their constituents. So if these giants can practice such social temperance, why can't we? The seduction of personal technology and social media was certainly still well beyond their reach, but their commitment to quiet retreat and contemplative reflection fuels the deeper thought and grander plans they were able to enact. Sometimes limiting what and to whom we have access delivers the greatest bounty.

☞ **FLAWS SHALL FLOURISH.** From Larry Ellison to Helena Rubinstein, we've covered larger-than-life characters of mythic proportion. But perhaps their greatest trait of all is their humanity. They are all real, multidimensional, flawed humans—which contributes to their complexity. Greatness stems from adversity, not perfection. And flattening who you are to maintain the status quo will leave you somewhere in a murky sea of cool indifference. It's our rough edges that make us stronger and better and nudge us to be bolder than we thought imaginable.

☞ **TO SERVE OTHERS IS TO SERVE YOURSELF.** You need not be a philanthropist like Andrew Carnegie to live a life of service. At their core, innovators and entrepreneurs are public servants—or at least they have the power to be. Ambition and altruism need not be at odds. Not only can they coexist, they can be powerful complements. What will be your legacy? Eleanor Roosevelt writes, "The one sure way not to be happy is deliberately to map out a way of life in which one would please oneself completely and exclusively. For what keeps our interest in life and keeps us looking forward to tomorrow is giving pleasure to other people."[11] A life made useful to others is a happy life.

I don't advocate for everyone to abandon their current lives and start a company. That would be disastrous and impractical. But you can still embrace the entrepreneurial mindset, not only in your professional life but in your romantic relationships; in the way you deal with money; in the way you make decisions and the routines you establish for yourself; in the hobbies you pursue and the internal life you lead. Living your life like a startup isn't about securing venture capital or accumulating millions of users or adding an IPO to your resume. It's about revamping how you live, not through grand feats or dramatic gestures but subtly, every day. It means giving up on perfection and disrupting mental models. It's a life of physical and virtual experimentation, with one eye on your audience and the other gazing inward. It champions hustling over planning and making a choice over relying on luck.

It's a life of ups and downs and constant change—and working through those vicissitudes, however awkwardly, is authentic. And it's enough.

It's never too late to startup your life. The innovator's spirit invites you to piece together an existence of partitioned identities, disparate interests, honed and burgeoning skill sets, and a hodgepodge of people accumulated along the way. It's not a neat and tidy formula; it's fluid, flexible, frequently messy, and usually unpredictable. Whether you work at a corporation, are still in school, or are inching closer to retirement, a life of entrepreneurial expeditions will make you happier. Now roll up your sleeves, get off the sidelines, and free fall into the arena of your own life. It might not be pretty, but it will be fun.

Notes

INTRODUCTION

1   Tim Worstall, "The US Is Becoming More European: Half of Adult Americans Are Now Single," *Forbes*, September 11, 2014, http://www.forbes.com/sites /timworstall/2014/09/11/the-us-is-becoming-more-european-half-of-adult -americans-are-now-single/ (accessed December 5, 2015).
2   Ed Yardeni, "More Selfie Households Who Rent (Excerpt)," Dr. Ed's Blog, Yardeni Research, Inc., July 23, 2015, http://blog.yardeni.com/2015/07/more-selfie -households-who-rent-excerpt.html (accessed May 24, 2016).
3   Synergy Services Corporation, "4 Significant Trends that Will Impact the Workplace in 2016," *Synergy Services Corporation*, November 10, 2015, http://www .synergyservicescorp.com/4-significant-trends-that-will-impact-the-workplace -in-2016/ (accessed December 5, 2015).
4   David Garner, "Survey Says: Body Image Poll Results," *Psychology Today*, February

1, 1997, https://www.psychologytoday.com/articles/199702/survey-says-body-image-poll-results (accessed December 5, 2015).

5   Ryan Pinkham, "80% of Smartphone Users Check Their Phones before Brushing Their Teeth and Other Hot Topics," *Constant Contact*, April 5, 2013, http://blogs.constantcontact.com/smartphone-usage-statistics/ (accessed December 5, 2015).

6   Eric Ries, *The Lean Startup: How Today's Entrepreneurs Use Continuous Innovation to Create Radically Successful Businesses* (New York: Crown Publishing Group, 2011), 3.

1. THE IMPERFECT PROTOTYPE

1   Daniel Roberts, "How Kevin Systrom Got Started," *Fortune*, October 10, 2014, http://fortune.com/2014/10/10/how-kevin-systrom-got-started/ (accessed December 5, 2015).

2   Darrell Etherington, "Thalmic Labs Raises $14.5M to Make the MYO Armband the Next Big Thing in Gesture Control," *TechCrunch*, June 5, 2013, http://techcrunch.com/2013/06/05/thalmic-labs-raises-14-5m-to-make-the-myo-armband-the-next-big-thing-in-gesture-control/ (accessed December 14, 2015).

3   Quoted in Andy Reinhardt, "Interview: 'There's Sanity Returning,' Steve Jobs," *Business Week*, May 25, 1998.

4   Ben Popper, "This Is What a $55,000 Kickstarter Potato Salad Party Looks Like," *The Verge*, October 1, 2014, http://www.theverge.com/2014/10/1/6880201/potato-stock-kickstarter-potato-salad-zack-danger-brown (accessed May 16, 2016).

5   Jacquelyn Smith, "The Happiest and Unhappiest Jobs in America," *Forbes*, March 22, 2013, http://www.forbes.com/sites/jacquelynsmith/2013/03/22/the-happiest-and-unhappiest-jobs-in-america/2/ (accessed December 5, 2015).

6   Guy Kawasaki, "Mantras Versus Missions," January 2, 2006, http://guykawasaki.com/mantras_versus_/ (accessed December 5, 2015).

7   Rob Thomas, "The Veronica Mars Movie Project," Kickstarter.com, https://www.kickstarter.com/projects/559914737/the-veronica-mars-movie-project (accessed December 5, 2015).

2. GET YOUR MIND RIGHT

1   Jordan Kassalow, "Founder's Story," VisionSpring, 2013, http://visionspring.org/founders-story/ (accessed December 13, 2015).

2   Vivek Wadhwa, Raj Aggarwal, Krisztina "Z" Holly, and Alex Salkever, "The Anatomy of an Entrepreneur: Making of a Successful Entrepreneur," Kauffman.org, November 2009, http://www.kauffman.org/~/media/kauffman_org/research%20reports%20and%20covers/2009/07/makingofasuccessfulentrepreneur.pdf (accessed December 5, 2015).

3   Lucius Annaeus Seneca, *Letters from a Stoic: Epistulae Morales, AD Lucilium*, trans. Richard Mott Gummere (Enhanced Media, originally published 1917, 1920, 1925).

4   Neale Donald Walsch, "Your Life Begins at the End of Your Comfort Zone," YouTube.com, uploaded October 5, 2011, https://www.youtube.com/watch?v=wQzDFjWPyf8 (accessed December 6, 2015).

5   Shel Silverstein, *A Light in the Attic, Special Edition* (New York: Evil Eye Music, HarperCollins Publishers, 1981).

6   Max Chafkin, "A Broken Place: The Spectacular Failure of the Startup That Was

Going to Change the World," *Fast Company*, April 7, 2014, http://www.fastcompany .com/3028159/a-broken-place-better-place, n.d. (accessed December 6, 2015).

7 Noam Wasserman, "How an Entrepreneur's Passion Can Destroy a Startup," *The Wall Street Journal*, August 25, 2014, http://www.wsj.com/articles/how-an -entrepreneur-s-passion-can-destroy-a-startup-1408912044 (accessed December 6, 2015).

8 Dorothy Tennov, *Love and Limerence: The Experience of Being in Love* (Lanham, MD: Scarborough House, 1979).

9 A. C. Cooper, C. Y. Woo, W. C. Dunkelberg, "Entrepreneurs' Perceived Chances of Success," *Journal of Business Venturing* 3 (1988): 97–108.

10 BBC News, "Experts Debate Games Bid Benefits," *BBC News*, March 6, 2007, http://news.bbc.co.uk/2/hi/uk_news/scotland/glasgow_and_west/6422367 .stm (accessed December 6, 2015).

11 Michelle Roberts, "Tobacco 'Kills Two In Three Smokers," *BBC News*, February 24, 2015, http://www.bbc.com/news/health-31600118 (accessed December 6, 2015).

12 Jonny Cooper, "BASE Jumping: The Life-or-Death Appeal of the World's Most Dangerous Sport," *The Telegraph*, May 18, 2015, http://www.telegraph.co.uk/men /active/11612292/BASE-jumping-the-life-or-death-appeal-of-the-worlds-most -dangerous-sport.html (accessed December 6, 2015).

13 Claire Cain Miller, "The Divorce Surge Is Over, But the Myth Lives On," *The New York Times*, December 2, 2014, http://www.nytimes.com/2014/12/02/upshot/the -divorce-surge-is-over-but-the-myth-lives-on.html (accessed December 6, 2015).

14 Ibid.

15 Dr. Andreas Kappes and Dr. Tali Sharot, "Optimism and Entrepreneurship: A Double-edged Sword," *Nesta*, February 2015, http://affectivebrain.com/wp -content/uploads/2015/05/optimism_and_entrepreneurship_-_a_double -edged_sword.pdf (accessed December 6, 2015).

16 Sandra Aamodt, "Brain Maturity Extends Well Beyond Teen Years," interview by Tony Cox, NPR.org, October 10, 2011, http://www.npr.org/templates/story /story.php?storyId=141164708 (accessed December 6, 2015).

3. OUTSMART DUMB LUCK

1 Experiment details compiled from Thomas Eisenmann, Eric Ries, and Sarah Dillard, "Hypothesis-Driven Entrepreneurship: The Lean Startup," *Harvard Business School*, December 2011 (revised July 2013); Jennifer Hyman, Jennifer Fleiss, "Rent the Runway: From Idea to 750,000 Members," interview by Andrew Warner, Mixergy.com, March 16, 2011, http://mixergy.com/interviews/hyman -fleiss-rent-the-runway-interview/ (accessed December 6, 2015).

2 Leena Rao, "The Netflix for Designer Clothes, Rent the Runway Raises $20M from Vogue-Publisher Condé Nast and Kleiner Perkins," *TechCrunch*, November 30, 2012, http://techcrunch.com/2012/11/30/the-netflix-for-designer-clothes -rent-the-runway-raises-20m-from-vogue-publisher-conde-nast-and-kleiner -perkins/ (accessed December 6, 2015).

3 Jason Del Rey, "Rent the Runway Thinks Women Will Rent Everyday Cloth- ing. It's Now or Never," *Recode*, March 29, 2016, http://www.recode.net/2016/3

/29/11587318/rent-the-runway-thinks-women-will-rent-everyday-clothing-its
-now-or (accessed May 24, 2016).

4 Richard Wiseman, "The Luck Factor," *The Skeptical Inquirer* 27, no.3 (May/June
2003), http://www.richardwiseman.com/resources/The_Luck_Factor.pdf (accessed December 6, 2015).

5 Starbucks Newsroom, "Starbucks Details Five-Year Plan to Accelerate Profitable
Growth," *Starbucks Corporation*, December 4, 2014, https://news.starbucks.com
/news/starbucks-details-five-year-plan-to-accelerate-profitable-growth (accessed
December 6, 2015).

6 Associated Press, "Starbucks Names All 600 Stores to Be Closed," *USA Today*,
July 18, 2008, http://usatoday30.usatoday.com/money/industries/food/2008-07
-17-starbucks-closings_N.htm (accessed December 6, 2015).

7 Edison's Patents, *The Thomas Edison Papers*, Rutgers University, revised February 20, 2012, http://edison.rutgers.edu/patents.htm (accessed December 6, 2015).

8 B. C. Forbes, "Why Do So Many Men Never Amount to Anything?" *American
Magazine* (January 1921): 89.

4. EVERYTHING I NEED TO KNOW I UNLEARNED

1 "100 Fastest-Growing Companies," *Fortune*, 2009 http://archive.fortune.com
/magazines/fortune/fortunefastestgrowing/2009/snapshots/1.html (accessed
December 6, 2015).

2 IDC, "Smartphone OS Market Share, 2015, Q2," *IDC Research, Inc.*, http://www
.idc.com/prodserv/smartphone-os-market-share.jsp (accessed December 6, 2015).

3 Anthony Ramirez, "Blockbuster's Investing Led to Merger," *The New York Times*,
January 8, 1994, http://www.nytimes.com/1994/01/08/business/blockbuster-s
-investing-led-to-merger.html (accessed December 6, 2015).

4 "Fortune 500: Worst Stocks of 2010," *Fortune*, December 21, 2010, http://archive
.fortune.com/galleries/2010/fortune/1012/gallery.Fortune500_worst_stocks
.fortune/8.html (accessed December 13, 2015).

5 John A. Shedd, *Salt from My Attic* (Portland, ME: Mosher Press, 1928).

5. WIN EVERY ROOM

1 Nick Paumgarten, "The Merchant," *The New Yorker*, September 20, 2010, http://
www.newyorker.com/magazine/2010/09/20/the-merchant (accessed December
7, 2015).

2 Erika Adams, "Report: J. Crew Just Laid Off 10 Percent of Its Staff," Racked
.com, June 10, 2015, http://www.racked.com/2015/6/10/8761329/jcrew-layoffs
(accessed December 7, 2015).

3 Paumgarten, "The Merchant."

4 Ibid.

5 Google Mail, Google, 2015, https://plus.google.com/+Gmail/posts/AjktcDswdKh.

6 "Avon Founder David H. McConnell—Creating the Company for Women," Avon
Products, Inc., http://www.avoncompany.com/aboutavon/history/mcconnell.html
(accessed December 8, 2015).

7 "The Story of Wrigley," *Wm. Wrigley Jr. Company*, 2012, http://www.wrigley.com
/global/about-us/the-story-of-wrigley.aspx (accessed December 8, 2015).

8   Daniel J. Robinson, "Marketing Gum, Making Meanings: Wrigley in North America, 1890–1930," *Enterprise & Society* 5, no. 1 (March 2004): 4.

9   Christopher Warren-Gash, "Delivering Happiness: Why At Zappos It's Your Birthday Every Day," *Forbes*, May 31, 2012, http://www.forbes.com/sites/languatica/2012/05/31/delivering-happiness-why-at-zappos-its-your-birthday-every-day/ (accessed December 8, 2015).

10 Zappos.com, Inc., Zappos Milestone: Timeline, May 4, 2009, http://about.zappos.com/press-center/media-coverage/zappos-milestone-timeline (accessed December 8, 2015).

11 Tony Hsieh, "How Zappos Infuses Culture Using Core Values," *Harvard Business Review*, May 24, 2010, https://hbr.org/2010/05/how-zappos-infuses-culture-using-core-values (accessed December 8, 2015).

12 "Zappos' 10-Hour Long Customer Service Call Sets Record," *Huffington Post*, December 21, 2012, http://www.huffingtonpost.com/2012/12/21/zappos-10-hour-call_n_2345467.html (accessed December 8, 2015).

13 Tony Hsieh, "How I Did It: Zappos's CEO on Going to Extremes for Customers," *Harvard Business Review*, July-August 2010, https://hbr.org/2010/07/how-i-did-it-zapposs-ceo-on-going-to-extremes-for-customers (accessed December 8, 2015).

14 Ben Popken, "Zappos Saves Best Man from Going Barefoot at Wedding," *Consumerist*, May 19, 2011, http://consumerist.com/2011/05/19/zappos-saves-best-man-from-going-barefoot-at-wedding/ (accessed December 8, 2015).

15 Tony Hsieh, *Delivering Happiness: A Path to Profits, Passion, and Purpose* (Mundelein, IL: Round Table Comics, 2012).

16 Keith McFarland, "Why Zappos Offers New Hires $2,000 to Quit," *Bloomberg Business*, September 16, 2008, http://www.bloomberg.com/bw/stories/2008-09-16/why-zappos-offers-new-hires-2-000-to-quitbusinessweek-business-news-stock-market-and-financial-advice (accessed December 8, 2015)

17 Jerry Useem, "Are Bosses Necessary?" *The Atlantic,* October 2015, http://www.theatlantic.com/magazine/archive/2015/10/are-bosses-necessary/403216/ (accessed December 8, 2015).

18 Richard Feloni, "Inside Zappos CEO Tony Hsieh's Radical Management Experiment That Prompted 14% of Employees to Quit," *Business Insider,* May 16, 2015, http://www.businessinsider.com/tony-hsieh-zappos-holacracy-management-experiment-2015-5 (accessed December 8, 2015).

19 Rachel Emma Silverman, "At Zappos, Banishing the Bosses Brings Confusion," *The Wall Street Journal,* May 20, 2015, http://www.wsj.com/articles/at-zappos-banishing-the-bosses-brings-confusion-1432175402 (accessed December 8, 2015).

20 Design for Everyone, Inter-IKEA Systems B.V., 2015, http://www.ikea.com/ms/en_AU/this-is-ikea/democratic-design/index.html (accessed December 8, 2015).

6. WORK IT

1   Michael Gross, *Genuine Authentic: The Real Life of Ralph Lauren* (New York: HarperCollins Publishers, Inc., 2003).

2   Sadie Whitelocks, "Ralph Lauren's Rags to Riches: How Designer Went from being a Kid from the Bronx to a Fashion Mogul Worth $6.5 billion," *The Daily*

Mail, October 29, 2012, http://www.dailymail.co.uk/femail/article-2224914 /Ralph-Laurens-rags-riches-How-designer-went-kid-Bronx-fashion-mogul -worth-6-5billion.html (accessed December 8, 2015).

3 Ann L. Hollander, *Sex and Suits* (New York: Kodansha America, 1995).

7. GO VIRTUAL

1 Courtney Boyd Myers, "The Future According to Josh Harris. But Wait, Who's Josh Harris?" *The Next Web,* July 11, 2011, http://thenextweb.com/entrepreneur /2011/07/24/the-future-according-to-josh-harris-but-wait-whos-josh-harris/ (accessed December 8, 2015).

2 David Carr, "Sundance Toasts an Early Online Life," *The New York Times,* January 25, 2009, http://www.nytimes.com/2009/01/26/movies/26josh.html?_r=1 (accessed December 8, 2015).

3 Xeni Jardin, "Josh Harris: 'Pseudo Was a Fake Company,'" *BoingBoing,* June 26, 2008, http://boingboing.net/2008/06/26/josh-harris-pseudo-w.html (accessed December 8, 2015).

4 Boyd Myers, "The Future According to Josh Harris."

5 Allen Salkin, "For Him, the Web Was No Safety Net," *The New York Times,* August 29, 2009, http://www.nytimes.com/2009/08/30/fashion/30harris.html ?pagewanted=all, (accessed December 8, 2015).

6 Ondi Timoner, "Where Is Josh Harris Now? Catching Up With We Live in Public's Star Prophet 5 Years Later," *Huffington Post,* August 26, 2014 (accessed December 8, 2015).

7 Andrew Smith, "Josh Harris: The Warhol of the Web," *The Guardian,* November 4, 2009, http://www.theguardian.com/film/2009/nov/04/josh-harris-we-live -public (accessed November 27, 2015).

8 Marshall McLuhan, *Understanding Media* (Cambridge, MA: MIT Press, 1964), 7.

9 Caitlin Dewey, "Everyone You Know Will Be Able to Rate You on the Terrifying 'Yelp for People'—Whether You Want Them To or Not," *The Washington Post,* September 30, 2015, https://www.washingtonpost.com/news/the-intersect/wp /2015/09/30/everyone-you-know-will-be-able-to-rate-you-on-the-terrifying -yelp-for-people-whether-you-want-them-to-or-not/ (accessed November 27, 2015).

10 "Lulu App Just Got Infinitely More Guy-Friendly," *Huffington Post,* March 5, 2014, http://www.huffingtonpost.com/2014/03/05/lulu-app-changes-guy-friendly _n_4904748.html (accessed December 8, 2015).

11 Julia Cordray, "I Became a Trending Topic for the Wrong Reasons. Here's Why We Need Peeple, the Positivity App I'm Building," LinkedIn.com, October 4, 2015, https://www.linkedin.com/pulse/julia-cordray-ceo-peeple-creating-worlds -largest-app-julia-cordray (accessed December 8, 2015).

12 Bret Easton Ellis, "Bret Easton Ellis on Living in the Cult of Likability," *The New York Times,* December 8, 2015 (accessed December 13, 2015).

13 Charles Horton Cooley, *Human Nature and the Social Order* (New York: Scribner's, 1902), 152.

14 James Ball, "Silk Road: The Online Drug Marketplace That Officials Seem Powerless to Stop," *The Guardian,* March 22, 2013, http://www.theguardian

.com/world/2013/mar/22/silk-road-online-drug-marketplace (accessed May 9, 2016)

15 Joshuah Bearman, "The Rise and Fall of Silk Road, Part 1," *Wired Magazine,* April 2015, http://www.wired.com/2015/04/silk-road-1/ (accessed November 27, 2015).

16 Andy Greenberg, "'Silk Road 2.0' Launches, Promising a Resurrected Black Market for the Dark Web," *Forbes,* November 6, 2013, http://www.forbes.com /sites/andygreenberg/2013/11/06/silk-road-2-0-launches-promising-a -resurrected-black-market-for-the-dark-web/ (accessed December 8, 2015).

17 Sarah Jeong, "Silk Road Trial Closing Arguments: 'The Internet Permits Deception and Misdirection,'" *Forbes,* February 3, 2015, http://www.forbes.com /sites/sarahjeong/2015/02/03/silk-road-trial-closing-arguments-the-internet -permits-deception-and-misdirection/#4f1978f3601d (accessed May 9, 2016).

18 Kristina Dell, "How Second Life Affects Real Life," *Time,* May 12, 2008, http://content.time.com/time/health/article/0,8599,1739601,00.html (accessed December 8, 2015).

19 Mitra Ananda, *Digital Games: Computers at Play* (New York: Chelsea House Publishing, 2010).

20 Ed Diener and Martin Seligman, "Very Happy People," *Psychological Science* 13, no. 1 (January 2002), http://condor.depaul.edu/hstein/NAMGILES.pdf (accessed November 27, 2015).

21 Miller McPherson, Lynn Smith-Lovin, and Matthew E. Brashears, "Social Isolation in America: Changes in Core Discussion Networks over Two Decades," *American Sociological Review* 71, no. 3 (June 2006), http://asr.sagepub.com /content/71/3/353.short?rss=1&ssource=mfc (accessed November 27, 2015).

22 Maria Konnikova, "The Limits of Friendship," *The New Yorker,* October 7, 2014, http://www.newyorker.com/science/maria-konnikova/social-media-affect -math-dunbar-number-friendships (accessed November 27, 2015).

23 Seth Godin, *E-Mail Addresses of the Rich and Famous* (New York: Addison-Wesley, 1994).

24 Helen A. S. Popkin, "Getting the Skinny On Twitter's 'Cisco Fatty,'" *NBCNEWS .com,* March 27, 2009, http://www.nbcnews.com/id/29901380/ns/technology _and_science-tech_and_gadgets/t/getting-skinny-twitters-cisco-fatty /#.VlkTxGSrRbU (accessed November 27, 2015).

25 Easton Ellis, "Bret Easton Ellis on Living in the Cult of Likability."

26 Zygmunt Bauman, *Consuming Life* (Cambridge, UK: Polity Press, 2007).

27 Rachel McNeil, "Houston Plastic Surgeon Develops 'Facebook Facelift,' KPRC .com, August 3, 2015, http://www.click2houston.com/news/houston-plastic -surgeon-develops-facebook-facelift/34503376 (accessed November 27, 2015).

8. HUSTLE AND GROW

1 "Larry Ellison Interview," Academy of Achievement, May 22, 1997, http://www .achievement.org/autodoc/page/ell0int-1 (accessed May 9, 2016).

2 Adam Cohen, "Speak Oracle," *The New York Times,* February 15, 2004, http:// www.nytimes.com/2004/02/15/books/speak-oracle.html (accessed December 9, 2015); "The World's Billionaires," December 9, 2015, *Forbes,* http://www.forbes .com/profile/larry-ellison/ (accessed December 9, 2015).

3   Madeline Stone, "Larry Ellison's $300 Million Hawaiian Island Is Home to 400 Feral Cats," *Business Insider*, August 23, 2015, http://www.businessinsider.com /larry-ellisons-300-million-hawaiian-island-is-home-to-400-feral-cats-2015-8 (accessed December 9, 2015).

4   David Nasaw, *Andrew Carnegie* (New York: The Penguin Press, 2006), 65.

5   Andrew Carnegie, *The Autobiography of Andrew Carnegie and the Gospel of Wealth* (New York: Signet Classics 2006).

6   Andrew Carnegie, *Wealth* (Cedar Falls, IA: University of Northern Iowa, North American Review, 1889).

7   Ibid.

8   Carnegie, *Autobiography of Andrew Carnegie*.

9   Mark Zuckerberg, "A Letter to Our Daughter," www.facebook.com, December 1, 2015, https://www.facebook.com/notes/mark-zuckerberg/a-letter-to-our -daughter/10153375081581634 (accessed December 9, 2015).

10 Andrew Carnegie, "Mr. Carnegie's Address," *Presentation of the Carnegie Library to the People of Pittsburgh, with a Description of the Dedicatory Exercises, November 5th, 1895* (Pittsburgh: Order of the Corporation of the City of Pittsburgh, 1895), 13–14.

11 P. Brickman, D. Coates, and R. Janoff-Bulman, "Lottery Winners and Accident Victims: Is Happiness Relative?" *US National Library of Medicine National Institutes of Health* (August 1978), http://www.ncbi.nlm.nih.gov/pubmed/690806 (accessed December 9, 2015).

12 Elizabeth W. Dunn, Lara B. Aknin, and Michael I. Norton, "Spending Money on Others Promotes Happiness," *Science* 319, no. 5870 (March 2008): 1687–1688.

13 Dorothy Watson, Florian Pichler, and Claire Wallace, "Second European Quality of Life Survey: Subjective Well-Being in Europe," *European Foundation for the Improvement of Living and Working Conditions* (2010), http://www.eurofound.europa .eu/sites/default/files/ef_publication/field_ef_document/ef09108en.pdf (accessed November 18, 2015).

14 Dunn, Aknin, and Norton, "Spending Money on Others Promotes Happiness."

15 Nathan McAlone, "Bootstrapped Dating Site PlentyOfFish Has Fewer than 100 Employees and Match Just Bought It for $575 Million in Cash," *Business Insider*, July 14, 2015, http://www.businessinsider.com/match-buys-plentyoffish-for-575 -million-2015-7 (accessed December 9, 2015).

16 Alyson Shontell, "Now-Massive Companies That Didn't Need Venture Capital to Get Off the Ground," *Business Insider*, October 1, 2012, http://www .businessinsider.com/bootstrapped-companies-2012-10.

17 Tom Foster, "Building a Company the Hard Way," *Inc. Magazine*, September 2014, http://www.inc.com/magazine/201409/tom-foster/inc.500-companies -who-bootrapped-their-way-to-success.html (accessed December 9, 2015).

18 Elon Musk, interview by Chris Anderson, *TED Talks*, February 2013, https:// www.ted.com/talks/elon_musk_the_mind_behind_tesla_spacex_solarcity ?language=en (accessed December 9, 2015).

19 "Bill Gates 2.0," interview by Charlie Rose, *60 Minutes*, May 21, 2013, http:// www.cbsnews.com/news/bill-gates-20-21-05-2013/ (accessed December 9, 2015).

20 Penelope Green, "Where Tiny Houses and Big Dreams Grow," *The New York Times*, September 23, 2015, http://www.nytimes.com/2015/09/24/fashion/the -cabin-porn-commune.html?_r=0 (accessed December 9, 2015).

21 Matthew R. Durose, Alexia D. Cooper, and Howard N. Snyder, "Recidivism of Prisoners Released in 30 States in 2005: Patterns from 2005 to 2010," Bureau of Justice Statistics Special Report, April 2014, NCJ 244205, www.bjs.gov/content /pub/pdf/rprts05p0510.pdf. Seventy-five percent recidivism is after five years post-release.

9. THE PARTNERSHIP PUZZLE

1 Louise Story, "Can Burt's Bees Turn Clorox Green?" *The New York Times*, January 6, 2008, http://www.nytimes.com/2008/01/06/business/06bees.html (accessed December 9, 2015).

2 Richard L. Brandt, *One Click: Jeff Bezos and the Rise of Amazon.com* (New York: Penguin Group, 2011).

3 Tara Parker-Pope, "A New Risk Factor: Your Social Life," *The New York Times*, July 28, 2010, http://well.blogs.nytimes.com/2010/07/28/a-new-risk-factor-your -social-life/ (accessed December 9, 2015).

4 Name changed.

5 Larry Magid, "A Third of Recently Married Couples Met Online and They're More Satisfied and Less Likely To Split-Up," *Forbes*, June 3, 2013, http://www .forbes.com/sites/larrymagid/2013/06/03/a-third-of-recently-married-couples -met-online-and-theyre-more-satisfied-and-less-likely-to-split-up/ (accessed December 9, 2015).

6 Name changed.

7 Neil Strauss, *The Game* (New York: HarperCollins Publishers, 2005).

8 Molly E. Ireland, Richard B. Slatcher, Paul W. Eastwick, Lauren E. Scissors, Eli J. Finkel, and James W. Pennebaker, "Language Style Matching Predicts Relationship Initiation and Stability," *Psychological Science* 22, no. 1 (January 2011): 39–44.

9 Linda A. Jackson, John E. Hunter, and Carole N. Hodge, "Physical Attractiveness and Intellectual Competence: A Meta-Analytic Review," *Social Psychology Quarterly* 58, no. 2 (June 1995): 108–122.

10 Drew Grant, "The Paul Janka Experience: New York's PUA Poster Boy Makes Cash Money, Infomercials (Video)," *The Observer*, February 5, 2013, http:// observer.com/2013/02/the-paul-janka-experience-new-yorks-pua-poster-boy -makes-cash-money-infomercials-video/ (accessed December 9, 2015).

11 Paul Janka, telephone interview by Anna Akbari, July 28, 2014.

12 Ibid.

13 Thomas Edwards, telephone interview by Anna Akbari, July 28, 2014.

14 Evan Katz, telephone interview by Anna Akbari, July 22, 2014.

15 *Kate & Leopold*, directed by James Mangold (2001; Santa Monica, CA: Miramax, 2002), DVD.

16 Jeremy Nicholson, "Why You Shouldn't Believe in Soul Mates," *Psychology Today*, July 10, 2012, https://www.psychologytoday.com/blog/the-attraction-doctor /201207/why-you-shouldnt-believe-in-soul-mates (accessed December 9, 2015).

17 C. R. Knee, "Implicit Theories of Relationships: Assessment and Prediction of Romantic Relationship Initiation, Coping, and Longevity," *Journal of Personality and Social Psychology* 74 (1998): 360–370.

18 Name changed.

19 Name changed.

20 Mihaly Csikszentmihalyi, *Flow: The Psychology of Optimal Experience* (New York: HarperCollins Publishers, 1991), 103.

21 Elizabeth Gilbert, *Committed: A Love Story* (London: Bloomsbury Publishing, 2010), 79.

22 Criss Jami, *Venus in Arms* (United States: Criss Jami, 2012), 2.

23 "Michael Eisner Finds the Magic in Partnership from Bill and Melinda to Buffett and Munger," *The Telegraph*, October 9, 2010, http://www.telegraph.co.uk /finance/financetopics/profiles/8051241/Michael-Eisner-finds-the-magic-in -partnership-from-Bill-and-Melinda-to-Buffett-and-Munger.html (accessed November 25, 2015).

24 Adam Bryant, "Gary Smith of Ciena: Build a Culture on Trust and Respect," *The New York Times*, October 3, 2015, http://www.nytimes.com/2015/10/04 /business/gary-smith-of-ciena-build-a-culture-on-trust-and-respect.html?_r=0 (accessed November 25, 2015).

25 Arthur C. Brooks, "Taking Risks in Love," *The New York Times*, February 13, 2015, http://www.nytimes.com/2015/02/14/opinion/arthur-c-brooks-taking -risks-in-love.html?_r=1 (accessed November 25, 2015).

10. BELLYFLOP WITH GRACE

1 Rovio Entertainment Ltd., Press section, "1 Billion Angry Birds Downloads!" September 5, 2012, http://www.rovio.com/en/news/blog/162/1-billion-angry -birds-downloads (accessed November 24, 2015); Paul Kendall, "Angry Birds: The Story behind iPhone's Gaming Phenomenon," *The Telegraph*, February 7, 2011, http://www.telegraph.co.uk/technology/video-games/8303173/Angry -Birds-the-story-behind-iPhones-gaming-phenomenon.html (accessed November 24, 2015).

2 J. M. Barrie, *The Little Minister* (London: Cassell and Company Ltd., 1893), 24.

3 Dave McClure, "What Startups Failed because They Weren't 'in the Right Place at the Right Time'?" *Quora.com*, May 21, 2013, https://www.quora.com/What -startups-failed-because-they-werent-in-the-right-place-at-the-right-time (accessed December 13, 2015).

4 Henry Ford, *My Life and Work—An Autobiography of Henry Ford* (Snowball Publishing, 2012); and Steven Watts, *The People's Tycoon: Henry Ford and the American Century* (New York: Vintage Books, 2005).

5 Bessemer Venture Partners, "The Anti-Portfolio," Bessemer Ventures, https:// www.bvp.com/portfolio/anti-portfolio (accessed December 10, 2015).

6 Jessica Salter, "Airbnb: The Story behind the $1.3bn Room-Letting Website," *The Telegraph,* September 7, 2012, http://www.telegraph.co.uk/technology/news /9525267/Airbnb-The-story-behind-the-1.3bn-room-letting-website.html (accessed December 10, 2015).

7 Scott Austin, "Airbnb: From Y Combinator to $112M Funding in Three Years," *The Wall Street Journal,* July 25, 2011, http://blogs.wsj.com/venturecapital/2011 /07/25/airbnb-from-y-combinator-to-112m-funding-in-three-years/ (accessed December 10, 2015).

8   Telis Demos, "Airbnb Raises $1.5 Billion in One of Largest Private Placements," *The Wall Street Journal,* June 26, 2015, http://www.wsj.com/articles/airbnb-raises -1-5-billion-in-one-of-largest-private-placements-1435363506 (accessed December 10, 2015).

9   Nancy Harrison, "Susan Lucci, 11 Times a Nominee, 8 Times a Bride, Up for Emmy Again," *The New York Times,* June 23, 1991, http://www.nytimes.com/1991 /06/23/nyregion/susan-lucci-11-times-a-nominee-8-times-a-bride-up-for -emmy-again.html (accessed December 10, 2015).

10 Lucci hosted *Saturday Night Live* on October 6, 1990, and she hosted the 20th Annual Daytime Emmy Awards in 1993. Jill Gerston, "TELEVISION; Susan Lucci Proves Winning Isn't Everything," *The New York Times,* May 23, 1993, http:// www.nytimes.com/1993/05/23/arts/television-susan-lucci-proves-winning-isn -t-everything.html (accessed December 10, 2015).

11 Jon Hamm, interview by Seth Meyers, *Late Night with Seth Meyers,* November 2, 2015.

12 Stu Woo, "Against the Wind, One of the Greatest Comebacks in Sports History," *The Wall Street Journal,* February 28, 2014, http://www.wsj.com/articles/SB1000 14240527023033938045793128039078497 (accessed December 10, 2015).

13 Jonathan Haidt, *The Happiness Hypothesis: Finding Modern Truth in Ancient Wisdom* (New York: Basic Books, 2006).

14 James W. Pennebaker, *Opening Up: The Healing Power of Expressing Emotions* (New York: The Guilford Press, 1997).

11. PEACE OUT AND LEVEL UP

1   Christopher Steiner, "Meet the Fastest Growing Company Ever," *Forbes,* August 12, 2010, http://www.forbes.com/forbes/2010/0830/entrepreneurs-groupon -facebook-twitter-next-web-phenom.html (accessed December 9, 2015).

2   Nicholas Carlson, "Yahoo's Informal Offer to Buy Groupon: $3 Billion To $4 Billion," *Business Insider,* November 9, 2010, http://www.businessinsider.com /yahoo-hints-at-3-billion-offer-for-groupon-2010-11 (accessed November 25, 2015).

3   Mike Isaac, "Groupon Turns Down Google's $6 Billion Offer," *Forbes,* December 10, 2010, http://www.forbes.com/sites/mikeisaac/2010/12/03/groupon -turns-down-googles-6-billion-offer/ (accessed December 9, 2015).

4   Frank Sennett, "Behind Groupon's $6 Billion Brushoff," *The Wall Street Journal,* June 5, 2012, adapted from Frank Sennett, *Groupon's Biggest Deal Ever* (New York: St. Martin's Press, 2012), http://www.wsj.com/articles/SB100014240527 02303640104577440580610986086 (accessed December 13, 2015).

5   Herb Greenberg, "Greenberg: Worst CEO of 2012," *CNBC.com,* December 18, 2012, http://www.cnbc.com/id/100320782 (accessed December 9, 2015).

6   Walter Pavlo, "Groupon Accounting Scandal, and We're Surprised?" *Forbes,* April 3, 2012, http://www.forbes.com/sites/walterpavlo/2012/04/03/groupon -accounting-scandal-and-were-surprised/ (accessed December 9, 2015).

7   "Groupon Announces Revised Fourth Quarter and Full Year 2011 Results, Confirms First Quarter Guidance," Groupon, Inc., March 30, 2012, http://investor .groupon.com/releasedetail.cfm?releaseid=660861 (accessed December 9, 2015).

8   "The Unicorn List: Current Private Companies Valued At $1B And Above," *CB Insights,* https://www.cbinsights.com/research-unicorn-companies (accessed December 9, 2015).

9   Stephanie S. Spielmann, Geoff MacDonald, Jessica A. Maxwell, Samantha Joel, Diana Peragine, Amy Muise, and Emily A. Impett, "Settling for Less Out of Fear of Being Single," *Journal of Personality and Social Psychology* 105, no. 6 (Dec 2013): 1049–1073.

10 Connel Forrest, "How the 'PayPal Mafia' Redefined Success in Silicon Valley," *TechRepublic,* June 30, 2014, http://www.techrepublic.com/article/how-the -paypal-mafia-redefined-success-in-silicon-valley/ (accessed November 25, 2015).

11 Nate Davis, "Saints' Win Over Colts In Super Bowl XLIV Is Most-Watched Television Program Ever," *USA Today,* February 8, 2010, http://content.usatoday .com/communities/thehuddle/post/2010/02/saints-win-in-super-bowl-xliv -scores-highest-tv-ratings-since-1987/1#.Vmj1MWQrL_R (accessed November 25, 2015).

12 Arie W. Kruglanski and Donna M. Webster, "Motivated Closing of the Mind: 'Seizing' and 'Freezing,'" American Psychological Association, *Psychological Review* 103, no. 2 (April 1996): 263–283.

13 William Bridges, *Transitions: Making Sense of Life's Changes*, rev. 25th anniversary ed. (Cambridge, MA: Da Capo Press, 2004).

14 William Bridges, *The Way of Transition: Embracing Life's Most Difficult Moments* (New York: Perseus Publishing, 2001).

15 *Back to the Future,* dir. Robert Zemeckis (1985; Universal City, CA: Universal Pictures, 2002), DVD.

16 Gretchen Rubin, *Better Than Before: Mastering the Habits of Our Everyday Lives* (New York: Crown Publishers, 2015).

17 Joseph Campbell, *Reflections on the Art of Living: A Joseph Campbell Companion* (New York: HarperCollins Publishers, 1991).

18 Joseph Campbell, *The Power of Myth* (New York: Anchor Books, 1991).

12. HITTING REFRESH

1   Adam L. Penenberg, "An Insider's History of How a Podcasting Start-up Pivoted to Become Twitter," *Fast Company,* August 9, 2012, http://www.fastcompany .com/1837848/insiders-history-how-podcasting-startup-pivoted-become -twitter (accessed November 27, 2015).

2   Laurie Segall, "Early Twitter Employees to Miss Out On Millions," *CNNMoney,* September 26, 2013, http://money.cnn.com/2013/09/26/technology/social /twitter-ipo-stock/ (accessed November 27, 2015).

3   Robin Wauters, "First Public Tweet Sent Six Years Ago Today," *The Next Web,* March 21, 2012, http://usatoday30.usatoday.com/tech/news/story/2012-03-21 /twitter-birthday/53684356/1 (accessed November 27, 2015).

4   Jim Hopkins, "Surprise! There's a Third YouTube Co-Founder," *USA Today,* October 11, 2006, http://usatoday30.usatoday.com/tech/news/2006-10-11 -youtube-karim_x.htm (accessed November 27, 2015).

5   J. D. Alois, "Soylent. Spend Less Time Eating So You Can Spend More Time Working," *Crowdfund Insider,* June 14, 2015, http://www.crowdfundinsider.com

/2015/06/69482-soylent-spend-less-time-eating-so-you-can-spend-more-time
-working/ (accessed December 9, 2015).

6   Johan Huizinga, *Homo Ludens: A Study of the Play-Element in Culture* (Boston: Beacon Press, 1955).

7   Al Gore and Tipper Gore, *Joined at the Heart: The Transformation of the American Family* (New York: Henry Holt and Company, 2002).

8   Ludwig Wittgenstein, *Culture and Value* (Chicago: University of Chicago Press, 1980).

9   The phrase "enchanted objects" is inspired by David Rose, *Enchanted Objects: Innovation, Design, and the Future of Technology* (New York: Scribner, 2015).

10   Vivek Wadhwa, "When It Comes to Founding Successful Startups, Old Guys Rule," *TechCrunch*, September 7, 2009, http://techcrunch.com/2009/09/07/when-it-comes-to-founding-successful-startups-old-guys-rule/ (accessed December 9, 2015).

11   Michèle Fitoussi, *Helena Rubinstein: The Woman Who Invented Beauty* (Paris: Bernard Grasset, 2010).

12   Ibid.

13   Lindy Woodhead, *War Paint: Madame Helena Rubinstein and Miss Elizabeth Arden, Their Lives, Their Times, Their Rivalry* (Hoboken: John Wiley & Sons, 2003).

14   Nancy F. Koehn, *Brand New: How Entrepreneurs Earned Consumers' Trust from Wedgwood to Dell* (Cambridge, MA: Harvard Business School Publishing, 2001).

15   Jelaluddin Rumi, *Rumi's Little Book of Life: The Garden of the Soul, the Heart, and the Spirit*, trans. Maryam Mafi and Azima Melita Kolin (Charlottesville, VA: Hampton Roads Publishing Company, 2012).

16   Jelaluddin Rumi, "The Window Between Hearts," *The Rumi Collection*, edited by Kabir Helminski (Boston, MA: Shambhala Publications, 1998).

17   C. S. Lewis, *The Lion, the Witch and the Wardrobe; A Story for Children* (London: G. Bies Publishers, 1950).

18   Sławomir Mrożek, *Male Listy* (Warsaw: Noir Sur Blanc, 2002).

19   Dwight Garner, "Inside a Conjurer of Characters, 'Tibetan Peach Pie,' a Tom Robbins Memoir," *The New York Times*, May 20, 2014, http://www.nytimes.com/2014/05/21/books/tibetan-peach-pie-a-tom-robbins-memoir.html (accessed December 9, 2015).

20   Voltaire, *Voltaire's Philosophical Dictionary* (New York: Carlton House, Amazon Digital Services, 2012).

21   Louis Brown, *A Radar History of World War II: Technical and Military Imperatives* (New York: Taylor & Francis Group, LLC, 1999).

CONCLUSION: FREE FALLING IN THE ARENA

1   Candice Millard, *River Of Doubt: Theodore Roosevelt's Darkest Journey* (New York: Broadway Books, 2005).

2   Ibid.

3   Theodore Roosevelt, "The Strenuous Life Speech," April 10, 1899, Chicago, Illinois.

4   Theodore Roosevelt, "Citizenship in a Republic Speech," April 23, 1910, Sorbonne, Paris, France.

5   Roosevelt, "The Strenuous Life Speech."

6 *The Roosevelts: An Intimate History,* dir. Ken Burns (2014; Walpole, NH: Florentine Films, 2014), DVD.

7 Annie Dillard, *The Writing Life* (New York: Harper & Row, Publishers, Inc., 1989), 32.

8 Reid Hoffman, co-founder of LinkedIn, interview by Emily Chang, *Bloomberg West,* May 9, 2002.

9 Eleanor Roosevelt, *You Learn by Living* (HarperCollins: New York, 1960), 41.

10 Joseph Campbell, *Pathways to Bliss: Mythology and Personal Transformation* (Novato, CA: New World Library, 2004), xxiv.

11 Roosevelt, *You Learn By Living,* 95.